THE REFLECTION PROCESS

IN

CASEWORK SUPERVISION

Janet Mattinson

GW00750574

INSTITUTE OF MARITAL STUDIES

The Tavistock Institute of Human Relations

ISBN 901882100

First Published 1975
Reprinted 1977
2nd Edition 1992

PRINTED IN GREAT BRITAIN BY HEADLEY BROTHERS LTD
109 KINGSWAY LONDON WC2B 6PX AND ASHFORD KENT

CONTENTS

page

Preface to Second Edition   5

Foreword   7

Chapter One   Introduction   11

Chapter Two   Basic Assumptions   23

Chapter Three   The Reflection Process   49

Chapter Four   Manifestations of the Reflection Process   49
  Example I   Either-Or   52
    Comment   69
    Postscript   73
    Summary   74

  Example II   The Problem of Belonging   77
    Two Months Later   88
    Comment   89
    Postscript   92
    Summary   93

  Example III   The Management of the Thumping   96
    Comment   102
    A Fortnight Later   103
    Comment   110
    Postscript   113
    Summary   114

  Example IV   A Three-Cornered Affair   116
    Comment   122
    Postscript   123
    Summary   124

Chapter Five   Application   127

Appendix One   Postscript on the Case of Jack and
                     Lorna Hill (continued)   139

Appendix Two   List of Supervisors who attended Seminars
                     on "Processes of Interaction", 1965
                     to 1974   143

References   147

PREFACE TO THE SECOND EDITION

The second edition of this classic social work text is made in response to the continuing demand from social workers, counsellors and other practitioners who, as supervisors, or even as supervisees, want to learn more about their (sometimes unwitting and unconcious) involvement in the emotional worlds of their clients and how to use this experience productively.

Practitioners not only influence but are also influenced by their clients in the process of offering help. The 'push-me-pull-you' dynamics of client-worker interactions are never stronger than when helping society's most vulnerable individuals: abused or at risk children, the mentally ill, the disabled and the infirm elderly. While better services require enlightened legislation and efficient administrative guidelines, countless public enquiries affirm that these are not in themselves sufficient.

The Reflection Process offers a psychological explanation of how practitioners become caught up in the problems they try to resolve. While an awareness of the process can be used inappropriately to justify bad practice, used sensitively it has the potential to increase the understanding of complex processes of interaction and provides an invaluable working guide through freeing supervisees and supervisors from dysfunctional collusive behaviour with each other and their clients.

ACKNOWLEDGEMENTS

In the first chapter of this book, I describe how the social workers in Devon, supervising students on the graduate social work course at the University of Exeter, pushed the Institute of Marital Studies into thinking about the difficult task of supervision, and then, with my colleagues and me developed a way of working which led to the ideas expressed in this book. The supervisors and members of the University and I.M.S. staff are listed in Appendix One. On behalf of us all, contributors in one way or another to this book, I thank Professor Duncan Mitchell and the principal officers of Devon and Plymouth, and later Somerset, who supported the workshop by granting facilities and seconding and financing members.

Other social workers who have attended I.M.S. courses on supervision have also contributed and are also listed. They will recognise their own contributions in two of the examples given in Chapter Four. Two of these courses were financed by the London Boroughs' Training Committee.

I particularly want to thank the supervisors, workers and students who gave me permission to use their detailed work in Chapters One and Four. I could not have asked them if their work had not been of well above average ability. For people of less professional competence and confidence, this detailed exposure of work would have been too difficult.

My colleagues referred to in the text are Miss Clemency Chapman, Mrs Patricia Coussell and Mr Douglas Woodhouse, and I think they know how much I have enjoyed working with them at Exeter and in London. Many of my other colleagues have commented on the script. Mrs Ann Bernabo and Mrs Linda Besharat, secretaries at different times in the Institute, typed parts of the text. Mrs Shirley Palmer struggled with and managed to transcribe the tape-recordings of the seminars, only occasionally pleading with me to ask members "not all to speak at the same time".

I extend my thanks to the authors and the English and American publishers who have given me permission to quote the lengthier extracts from copyright material, but, especially, I want to thank Dr Harold Searles whom I mainly quote and whose title, *The Reflection Process*, and definitions I have used.

And, of course, all the contributors and I thank the clients (their identity is concealed) who, by their words and actions, told us of their difficulties and taught us, as long as we could spare the time to listen to them, more than we could teach ourselves.

FOREWORD

It is with great pleasure that I am writing a foreword for this new edition of Janet Mattinson's classic monograph on The Reflection Process in Casework Supervision. I find that most of what I wrote in 1975 still holds true. This monograph grew out of an interaction between practice and teaching and followed the tradition, set by the Tavistock Institute of Marital Studies, that written work should arise from and relate back to work with users. In the Institute's work and in this book theory and practice, thinking and feeling, are held together. The Institute, and Janet Mattinson herself, made a major contribution to this unity by their insistence that the knowledge and understanding required to help people who suffered from marital problems was to be found by studying the relationships between partners rather than the individuals themselves. Their earlier publications had shown the value of studying the interactions and cross currents between partners in a marriage and between those partners and their caseworkers. This monograph pinpoints, and then offers an explanation for, another phenomenon of interrelationships: that the worker-client relationship and the worker-supervisor relationship will sometimes mirror each other; the one making clearer what is happening in the other. The bridge between these relationships is the open, flexible and penetrable internal world of the social worker. This is an important and logical extension of the Institute's belief that relationships are not discrete, but form a seamless web, stretching out in an ever extending network. In this monograph Janet Mattinson explores one section of this web, suggesting that its filaments are made of transference and counter transference.

In doing so she explores ideas about the desirable distance between worker and client and states clearly and unequivocally that to help another person one has to be involved. This is perhaps even more important today than when the monograph was first written. There is a real danger that a combination of larger organisations, increasingly stressful work, a hostile media and staff shortages are resulting in a flight by social workers from their users. They can find refuge from involvement in procedures and bureaucratic structures and blame this upon their managers, and with considerable justification. But to help another person emotionally you must be close enough to care for, as well as about, them and such caring means involvement. Involvement is not of course entirely a matter of choice once one has exposed oneself to the possibility. It is also an unconscious process. Certainly one can control it a little by the frequency and place of meeting, but there is an unconscious element in client and in worker which largely determines the closeness of the relationship. This is neither good nor bad; it is a fact of human relationships. Janet Mattinson makes clear that it can become a useful tool only if the social worker is able to risk feeling and then to understand these feelings in order to bring what was unconscious into consciousness. To understand what you are feeling you have to take the risk of letting those feelings out and of behaving naturally and spontaneously with supervisors or groups of colleagues. Once you have experienced the feelings they can be understood, but to try to understand before feeling is a sterile and useless activity. The social workers and supervisors in the groups described by Janet Mattinson were brave enough to take the risk and because they were, we have another dimension for understanding each other.

The implications of this knowledge are far more numerous than I can see because they stretch outwards like ripples on a pond. I am sure however that they have implications beyond casework. From my own experience I know that when one supervises people working with groups, the worker who is describing his/her client group will often begin to behave like the group he is describing, while members of the supervising group act in the ways the worker maintains he behaved with his client group. As with casework supervisors this provides an additional dimension for understanding. The behaviour becomes part of the here and now and there is a chance to understand experientially and intellectually at the same time. Such complete understanding is the kind that can be used in practice because when you understand in this way you make the knowledge your own and it is no longer at one remove on paper or in another person.

There is no reason why the processes Janet Mattinson describes should be confined to therapeutic situations although they may be more readily recognised there. Management and teaching are both illuminated by the process of reflection. The management of the now large social services department might be considerably helped by an understanding of this process. Line management is almost by definition a vehicle for reflection and more attention to this dynamic might assist social services managers in the difficult but interesting task of managing people whose independence and professional judgement they must promote. Making use of this reflection would allow managers to give back to their staff the professional tools they need for their front line task and provides a defence against the 'managerialism' into which social services departments tend to lapse.

In my teaching career I have found that a knowledge of reflection has helped me to understand myself and my students and to make a conscious use of the possibilities inherent in it. In 1975 I wrote that reflection added to our meagre knowledge about supervision and went on to say that I hoped it might allow for some new thinking about supervision which seemed to be in a bad way at that time. Then too many social workers were supervising too many students too soon and with insufficient help from social work teachers. Things have not improved but there is reason to think that, with the introduction of accreditation for practice teachers, the future will be brighter. Good practice teachers need theoretical and practical insights and the reprinting of this book is particularly opportune for them. It addresses an area which is the special province of supervision in social work education, the exploration of the worker-user relationship, and offers a way of working on it by understanding the student-practice teacher interaction.

I have another reason for being pleased to write this foreword. It allows me to express my thanks to the Institute not only for their contribution to social work knowledge but to my personal learning. I have always believed that social work teachers should continue to practice and at one time the Institute enabled me to put my beliefs into action by inviting me to be an associate member of their staff. What I learned from the staff and from my clients was of lasting personal value to me. Looking back, however, I am sure that the Institute allowed me to work, and offered me the privilege of exciting supervision, not just for my benefit. They probably saw more clearly than I did, that I was a link in a chain, a strand in the seamless web. As a social work teacher I have close relationships with quite a number of students each year and these students have relationships with many practice teachers and users. I passed on some of the knowedge and understanding I gained at the Institute along this human chain.

Looking back I am puzzled by the fact that social work literature has made so little use of such an illuminating idea. I cannot explain this since it has had a powerful impact upon my own behaviour as a social work educator and manager. Perhaps it needs re-stating by this new edition. It comes at a time when new legislation demands that users be involved in assessing and planning their own needs for care and when parents are to be partners in much child care provision. User involvement and participation are difficult to achieve and need far more than good intentions to implement. The reflection process provides one way of exploring and monitoring the extent to which they are being achieved.

Phyllida Parsloe
Professor of Social Work
University of Bristol

CHAPTER ONE

INTRODUCTION

This book is about one aspect of casework supervision which appears to have been neglected in the social work literature in Great Britain today.

The thesis is simple. "The processes at work currently in the *relationship between* client and worker are often reflected in the *relationship between* worker and supervisor."[1]* This process was first named by Searles in 1955 and I shall use his term, *the reflection process*,[2] throughout the book. His thesis is simple, but the practice of using it is much more difficult.

In the Institute of Marital Studies we have only slowly discovered the need to pick up this reflection, or *mirroring*,† understand its implications and use it in our supervision of workers and in our supervision of supervisors. For a long time in our work with marriages we were concentrating on our emerging understanding of some of the most poignant facets of the interaction between the married pair which "got into" the interaction between the workers; for example, ". . . she felt very abashed, and ruefully they both realised how successfully Mr Lorenz had succeeded in splitting them off into the good who waited and the bad who did not tell. Miss B. had even acted this out for him and had gone along with an attempt to exclude Mrs A., not only from the work, but from knowing about the work, when these might have been the last two interviews."[3]‡

In some ways we did know about the reflection process in our own practice and in its expression in the weekly case conference of the Institute which all members of staff must attend. In Part III of *Marriage: Studies in Emotional Conflict and Growth*, first published in 1960, these weekly case conferences are described: ". . . in the middle of a bit of theorising a caseworker may be struck by the similarity between her own behaviour and that of a particular client whose elaboration of material may have seemed, at times, to be aimed at something other than an elucidation of his problem."[4] However we often denied this knowledge in our teaching practice. In 1963, when we were first asked

---

* In this quotation I have substituted the word "client" for "patient", and the word "worker" for "analyst". I have continued this practice throughout the book when quoting from the psychoanalytic literature.

† To reflect; to show the image (Concise Oxford Dictionary).

‡ We normally work within a structure of each partner of the marriage having his own worker, whether the work is done in single or joint interviews, or in a mixture of the two.

by the University of Exeter and the Devon supervisors to give a course on supervision, we refused, saying, "We have never been in a position to claim any special expertise in supervision. Why come to a shop for a commodity it has never advertised?"[5] If the social workers in Devon felt they needed additional help in extending their training skills, we could help them only to extend their *own* casework skills, emphasising a dictum of the Institute that a person's teaching can never extend beyond what he has experienced in his own practice. This does not mean that a good practitioner is necessarily a good teacher; teaching skills are also required. But it does mean that a bad or inexperienced practitioner can be only a faulty or very limited and unresourceful teacher.

In 1965, after continued negotiations, the Sociology Department of the University of Exeter, in conjunction with the Institute of Marital Studies, offered a course for supervisors of students in professional social work training. The course consisted of four working days a year, divided into two parts with an interval of several months. Members were asked to bring one of their on-going cases for presentation in the first part, to continue to work with it in the interval, and to bring this same case back to the second part, so that all predictions, ideas and findings could be tested against the reality of the present work. It was called a "three-year experimental course", and the employing authorities were asked to commit themselves to seconding for the whole period members who remained in the area.

This course fulfilled its name, and in the second year it started to change its character. The supervisors, it seemed, were determined to get their way and have their original request met. They started to present in the small group seminars the cases of the students whom they were supervising, although some time was retained for presenting their own work as well. This was never lost, but the preliminary letter to members which was sent out the following year invited them to bring either their own or their student's case material. Because the work was so exploratory, and because it was a joint endeavour of the course members, of the University staff, and of the I.M.S. representatives, it was decided in one of the plenary sessions, which often helped to take the work forward and to formulate what we were trying to do, that "course" was an inappropriate name. Among the membership it verbally became a "workshop", although on paper it still remained a course.

In 1967 the "experimental course" was discontinued and the employing authorities were notified that the University would, again in conjunction with the Institute of Marital Studies, offer another course. The description of its content shows the development that had taken place:

"Briefly this course will have a broader focus, that of processes of interaction, those within families and those within the teaching situation between supervisors and students. It will be open by invitation yearly to all workers who supervise students from this University, and to all members of the preceding year's course and the experimental one, as it is hoped to maintain a culture, although a flexible one, which will enable new members to participate more easily and which will help to produce a developing body of knowledge on this subject."

Under an umbrella title of "Processes of Interaction", we were concerned to try to understand some aspects of the interaction in a family, between members and with the worker, and some aspects of the interaction between the student and the supervisor. And then, almost by accident it seemed, we discovered that sometimes there was a connection. In one sense one can say that most strategic discoveries are made "by accident". But in another sense, the climate has to be right for that accident to be noticed and this in itself is no accident.* When we broadened our vision from "Marital Interaction" to "Processes of Interaction" within the family and within the working and the teaching situation, we established a climate in which we could no longer ignore what previously we had contrived to ignore. I think the establishment of this climate was influenced by our acute awareness of the difficulties in the interaction between the supervisors, the university staff and ourselves, which had caused so much discomfort.

In this climate we were able to start picking up some facets of what went on in the supervisory situation which appeared to reflect what was going on in the working situation. And this was often so in the cases which the supervisors chose to present in the seminars, because, and most appropriately, these were the cases and the supervisory situations with which they and the students were having the most difficulty.

The reflection process obviously works two ways, from the work to the supervision and from the supervision to the work. The common factor in the two situations and the link between them is the student. He is the carrier from one situation to another. Our learning was very muddled and very groping and probably different members of the workshop grasped the idea of the process more easily one way round than the other. I first became aware of the reflection of the supervision in the casework. I had previously observed that if I and other supervisors over-taught a student, that student often tended to teach his client. The model was unconsciously transferred. For me the excitement, after feeling very muddled, came with the idea of the behaviour of the student in the interactive situation with the supervisor, in front of the supervisor's own eyes, giving a clue, not just to his own inadequacies, but to the difficulties of the client, a presented model of what

* The establishment of the climate which enables the accidental discovery to be made is described very vividly by Watson in "The Double Helix"[6] and by Grey Walter in "The Living Brain".[7]

the client was trying to do in his relationship with the student. It could be used as a diagnostic aid to understanding what was going on in the case. How often, I wondered, had I maligned a student, attributing strange facets of his behaviour only to his own difficulties?

But perhaps even more important was the idea that the student's behaviour, affected by the client's disturbance or characteristic way of relating, would in its turn affect the supervisor. If the supervisor's behaviour was out of character as well, they might together be re-enacting the clients' difficulties of expression. Perhaps I had been maligning supervisors as well.

I will give two simple and blatant examples of this. The first is called *The Wasp*, the second *The Scribe*. *The Wasp* was presented at the end of the experimental course, and quoted by Mr Woodhouse in his introductory paper in the first year of the new course. *The Scribe* was presented in my small group three years later when I came back to the workshop (as it was by then officially called, even on paper) as a member of the I.M.S. staff, previously having attended as a member of the University staff. It is because these examples are so blatant that I can remember them. (At that time we did not tape-record the small group or plenary sessions.) But their blatancy is also an indicator of the progress of the group, and we were not yet ready to perceive and use any subtler manifestations. The first example seemed a real break-through for many of the original members; the connection was seen, although not fully understood. The second example was a re-establishment of this piece of learning for me on my return to this type of work.

The Wasp

The supervisor, one of the original members of the experimental course, and recognised by the group as a whole as one of the best caseworkers and supervisors amongst them, opened her presentation by saying that she felt very waspish with her student, who seemed very flat and lethargic and emotionally uninvolved with her cases. She was disappointed and worried by her inability to help this student. She did not feel her present attitude was the most helpful, but still found herself *stinging* the girl into activity in an attempt to bring her expected potential ability to life.

She then presented the most worrying and most time-consuming of the student's cases. At the beginning of the placement the boy client had been placed on probation for a quite trivial offence. From the beginning of the work it had been difficult for the supervisor to learn what, if anything, was happening in the relationships within the family and with the student. It seemed hardly possible that the family or the interviews could be as flat as the student described. Was it the case or was it the student who was so defended? Why was she so closed up and unable to let herself get more involved in what had seemed to be a fairly straight-forward and not too difficult case? Although always reserved, she had previously appeared to be of average ability, and had not shown this type of withdrawal in her previous placements.

Then the boy committed a second offence and, while he was on remand at home waiting for a Child Guidance appointment, it became clearer that the student was not getting in touch with the mother's anxiety, and was tending to write her off as the failure. But there seemed more need to get into the work. The supervisor stung the student into making more home visits, which the student was reluctant to do, and she questioned her piercingly in trying to help her enlarge her understanding of what might lie behind the second offence. The supervisor felt trapped by the student into a way of behaviour which did not feel right nor "like myself".

And then, before the Child Guidance appointment, the boy exploded into a violent outburst of serious crime. He was remanded in custody. The student seemed to be able to make more contact with him in the Remand Home, but, although she was much more concerned, she was unnecessarily sharp in what she said to him. The student was now being the wasp.

At the Court hearing the student was shattered when the mother and the child flew into each other's arms and totally and pointedly ignored her. At the same time as being so hurt, she was reassured that the child's latest offences had not destroyed the relationship with his mother. She was able to tell the supervisor all this and it was the next week that the supervisor presented this work to us. The mother and the student had at last reacted and seemed alive, but the supervisor was still worried about her supervision of this particular student, her own waspish behaviour, and the future work with this family.

The difficulties in this case and its supervision could have been discussed in various ways. They could have been discussed only in terms of the supervisor's behaviour: "good supervisors should not behave like wasps." Or they could have been discussed only in terms of the student's difficulties; generally, her work had been lethargic and this might have been due to other factors in her life. Or they could have been discussed only in terms of the case: what had been defended against which only started to come to life after the violence of the last offence? All these ways are valid, but ignore the fact of interactive behaviour and the effect one person has on another, which in its turn can affect yet another. We tried to combine the three ways, and we found connections. The waspishness in the supervision had been reflected in the casework. The defended anxiety of the family had got into the student, whose behaviour with the supervisor had reflected that of the mother with her. The child was reacting to something in the family which was very impervious; only the seriousness of his last offences had produced a reaction. Only the sting of the supervisor had galvanised the student. It was now easier to see the difficulty of the case and, measured against the supervisor's reaction and that of the child, feel the strength of the defence that nothing was wrong after the first offence, and therefore the strength of the anxiety that lay behind this denial. It was now less surprising that the student, generally frightened of her own involvement, overplayed her own defence even more strongly in this situation, and at the same time tried to convey through her actions in the supervisory situation what she could not put into words and what she could not start to understand. It was not surprising, if her supervisor over-reacted to her imperviousness by stinging, that she adopted a similar method. Nothing less seemed to penetrate.

At the time we discussed this we could see some of the connections, but not the exact meaning. But the limited discussion that we did have helped the supervisor to work with the student in a different way. More aware that her own behaviour reflected something in the case, she had acquired a little insight into how the clients behaved with each other. With much more confidence she was able to discuss with the student the difficulties they were having, relate this to the case and thereby take out the sting and accusation. The difficulty of getting into the work with this family became less the student's own problem, although, of course, still partially hers (for example, her general lethargy). When it was discussed in these terms, the student was then able to lessen her defences, which had been heightened by this particular case.

This illustration highlights two important aspects of the basic thesis: firstly, that the supervisor's emotion may have its source in the client/worker relationship and chiefly in the client, and is therefore a reflection; secondly, that some of the behaviour of the student in the supervisory period may be an unconscious attempt to show the supervisor the kind of behaviour which the client has been exhibiting to him, which he does not understand (because he is not conscious of what he has absorbed) and with which he is most in need of supervisory help; it may not be just his own idiosyncrasy.[8]

As Searles says, ". . . my experience in hearing numerous additional therapists present cases before groups has caused me to become slow in forming an unfavourable opinion of any therapist on the basis of his presentation of a case. With convincing frequency I have seen that a therapist who during an occasional presentation appears to be lamentably anxious, compulsive, confused in his thinking, or what not, actually is a basically capable colleague who, as it were, is trying unconsciously by his demeanour during the presentation, to show us a major problem-area in the therapy with his patient. The problem-area is one which he

cannot perceive objectively and describe to us effectively in words:
rather, he is unconsciously identifying with it and is in effect trying
to describe it by the way of his behaviour during the presentation."[9]
The second example illustrates these same points:

The Scribe

The clients were a mother and eight-year-old son. The mother herself
referred her son who, she said, was beyond her control. Her husband
had deserted some years previously. On her first unheralded visit to
the welfare department she was seen by the supervisor, who soon decided to limit his work on this first interview and immediately pass the
case to his new student on his first placement. A home visit by the
student was arranged for the following week. It would be the student's
first case and his first home visit on the placement.

The student had done the visit and there had been one supervisory
session on it. The supervisor reported his concern about the client
situation and about the student's ability to work with it. Presumably
he was wondering whether he had given the student a case too difficult
for him. He reported on the supervisory situation, what he thought
had been the student's mis-management of the interview, and how he
had *written* the student's report for the file. At this point in the seminar,
the group did not express surprise. No-one queried this action.

We then had a description of the interview, which had been a mobile
one and had taken place in most rooms of the house. It started in the
front parlour where the mother "entertained" the student, showing him
the family photograph album; the photographs were sunny and smiling.
It all seemed very remote from the complaints she had made in the
office the previous week. When the student was eventually able to get
a word in, he asked the whereabouts of the child. He was briefly
informed that he was hiding from the student, and was on the top shelf
of the larder. The mother had not been able to persuade him to come
down and could not reach him. She continued to entertain the student,
who then took things into his own hands and went into the kitchen.
He did not succeed in having any conversation with the child on the
top shelf, but he was a tall student and eventually his offer of a lift
down was accepted. The three of them returned to the sitting room,
where the mother continued to entertain and the child started to write
letters to his mother. The first one said, "Shit"; the second one said,
"You are shit"; and the third one said, "You are shit-shit". The
interview then moved upstairs and the child remained silent.

"What's going on?" the supervisor asked the group, continuing to
express anxiety that the student had not managed the interview
appropriately. But the group did not agree. They thought he had
reacted sensitively and that it had been to his credit that the child had

allowed himself to be lifted down from the top shelf and had then proceeded to express his anger so directly. They continued to try to understand what were the other messages behind all the actions presented to him. Then they became more alive to the reflection which had got into the supervisory session. Why was the supervisor also writing? Writing in the supervisory session. And writing the student's report? What was he taking over? Only then was it remembered that the student, in his mid-twenties, had an Honours degree in Psychology and had one year's previous experience as a trainee family caseworker. The expectation of his not being able to write a report for the case-file was not based on the reality of his educational standard and experience, which was more than that of many other students on the course.

"Do you always write your students' reports?" a member of the group asked. Well, now he came to think of it, the supervisor had never done so before. So what had got into him? And what had got into the student that he meekly allowed his supervisor to write his report? This must have been quite contrary to his expectation of training.

Again this could have been taken up by the group as poor supervision. But the important factor in this case, as in *The Wasp*, was that the supervisor had acted out of character. He was known by the group to be a very caring caseworker, particularly good with families who had multiple problems. He was known to be a conscientious and helpful supervisor. But these positive qualities of warmth, care and helpfulness had been overplayed in this one instance. The supervisory session had been as acted-out as the interview. The inappropriate behaviour in the supervision was a reflection of the behaviour in the interview. This was then discussed as a diagnostic indication of the feelings underlying the interaction between the mother and the child. What was the child carrying for the mother? While she had been so entertaining and so evasive, he had portrayed withdrawal and then controlled but fairly excessive belligerence. Despite her words, the mother had been less explicit than the child. Her words had amounted to very little. What had she, unconsciously, attempted to get across to the student, which he had not understood, so that he had had to re-enact it with his supervisor, pushing him into being the competent one who did the writing? Was it weakness, anxiety, confusion or shame which the student reflected? The discussion continued on this theme without much clarification.

The reflection, in this presentation, had been of the case in the supervision. At that particular workshop the group seemed to need to know it had also understood the reflection the other way round and had done its work for the year. In the following and last seminar of the workshop a case was brought back for its second presentation. In the first half of the workshop, the woman client in a wheelchair had been not only housebound, but roombound as well. Apparently she was doing nothing, and there was little activity either in the work by the student or in the supervision. In the ensuing discussion the group thought that there was a marital problem and that the husband played a part in keeping his wife so immobilised. The marital interaction was looked at in some depth. At this later seminar the supervisor reported back that the student had implied that the group was talking nonsense. But the supervisor had persisted in getting the student to think along these lines. Since then, the work had been more with the husband, who, it turned out, had welcomed the opportunity to talk about some of their difficulties, not just the practical ones. It seemed that the group had pushed the supervisor; the supervisor had pushed the student; the student had pushed the husband; and the husband was now pushing his wife round the village; she was propelling herself round the house and an application had been made for an electric car. On that occasion we said goodbye and left feeling good.

This workshop continued to express a great deal of ambivalence about this type of work, new members finding it difficult at their first attendance to understand what we were trying to do. We still spent some time on the supervisors' own cases, trying to understand the processes of interaction within the family and between the members of that family and the worker. We kept on going back to this, not only for new members, but for old as well. Even for the most experienced, constant practice in this way of working, using the wits of the whole group and refusing to let go when it became difficult, was necessary. Sometimes their cases were more difficult than those of their students. Because of the nature of their position, usually supervising both students and staff, continually supporting younger and less experienced colleagues, and getting little supervision themselves, they needed at least an occasional stimulus.

The workshop retained its original developmental character, not changing fast, but occasionally and slowly altering its slant. One of the main changes was in its timing. Despite the financial difficulties for the employing authorities of seconding members twice in one year, the dates were altered so that the first and second parts came within one student placement. We were then able to ensure that the same case came back with the same worker. Another main change was that supervisors began to bring the work of junior staff whom they were supervising. Because what has been said so far can apply to any supervised casework and not just to the inexperienced student, I will use the word "worker" in the text from now on, unless in a particular example the worker happens to be a student and some of the discussion is relevant to his student status.

The broadening of the supervisory field faced us with greater problems of confidentiality in the group. Many of the students whose work had been discussed were not known, not likely to be known, to other members; at the end of the training, they would be leaving the area. The discussion of work of junior colleagues, well known in the area, obliged the group to reconsider their stance on this perpetually difficult subject. Where was the line which would enable us to continue working and which would not abuse and misuse our colleagues? A lapse of confidentiality on the part of one member incensed the group and brought the subject out into the open again. It was eventually decided that the work of supervised staff should not be barred from our discussion; that the group would consider itself bound by the usual rules of confidentiality and would not repeat outside the group what was discussed within it; that only minimal details of the worker were required for the task in hand and these related to status and general work performance. But each member of the group had to carry his own responsibility for what he felt was appropriate and relevant information to disclose and should not opt out of this responsibility and embarrass and burden the group with information they would not wish to know, nor frustrate and render the group useless by withholding what were obviously strategic facts. This the group would not tolerate. In these situations the supervisor had to forego the opportunity of getting help with his supervisory problem. Most supervisors had adopted the practice of asking their student's permission before they brought their work, and they decided to extend this to their junior colleagues.

Although this subject was repeatedly brought up for discussion and clarified again as the membership changed, it appeared, apart from the one unfortunate lapse, to have been handled quite well. There was enough confidence around for students and workers to allow their cases to be brought for discussion, knowing that the supervisor was also exposing his part of the proceedings. This may have been due to the culture in the area and the length of time over the years, rather than in actual hours or days, that the workshop had taken in establishing this way of working.

By this time, however, the Institute of Marital Studies was not so chary of owning any knowledge which was relevant and directly related to supervision. It also made a change in its training policy; its limited resources would be best spent in training key personnel, who in their turn would be training basic-grade workers. Using the learning acquired at Exeter, an extra-mural course of weekly seminars, lasting over two years, was started in London in 1970 for supervisors. And in 1971 another similar course, although with a different structure, was started in the London Boroughs, under the aegis of their Training

Committee. In the first year the supervisors had to bring their own work, in the second year that of workers or students whom they supervised.

On these courses two years was found to be a very short time in which to grasp the idea of the reflection process and for members to be able to use it in their own practice. One group had an initial difficulty in exposing their supervision in detail. When they appeared to be more confident about this, they then "clobbered" their students and young workers with the "seminar at the Tavistock". What they actually said when asking permission to bring the case we do not know, but an erroneous and too powerful image of what went on in the group appeared in some instances to be inappropriately and over-weightily reflected in the subsequent work, until this was picked up and looked at within the group. The difference between this group and the Exeter one may have been that in the latter the group leaders were never, or only marginally, ahead of the group and the learning. Perhaps we over-taught this London group and tried to hurry what had been achieved so much more slowly in Exeter with some of the founder members remaining four or five years in the group.

In the other London group this was not a difficulty once the plunge had been taken and it had been learnt from experience that the members were not treated harshly when they dared to expose their supervisory work in detail. But there was another difficulty, and that was in terms of selecting appropriate cases for the task of the seminar. In some of the work the supervisors presented it was clear that the reflection was not of the case in the supervision, but of the consistent difficulties of the worker in a number of dissimilar cases. It was not easy for the group to resist a supervisor's request for help with this type of problem when it knew that many of its members were desperately short on their staff-establishment and needed all the help they could get in raising the lowest standard of work. But we were primarily interested in the more refined process of helping average or good workers, who are not normally afraid of their own involvement, in using that involvement in the most constructive way both for the client and for their own work satisfaction.

The rest of this monograph is mainly about the reflection of the case in the supervision. In some instances, however, the supervisor has the greatest difficulty when the reflection of the case compounds what is either a real, or a felt, difficulty in his immediate working relationships which he has been unable to solve satisfactorily. The difficulty in the case and the difficulty in the formal and informal working structure then become very confused. I have included one example of this.

In this introduction, in the statement of the thesis and in the brief examples given, lie some big theoretical assumptions. In the next chapter I discuss these assumptions. In the third chapter I explain my own understanding of the reflection process in more detail and I describe some of the different manifestations which I have noticed. In this and the following chapter it becomes clear that there is no one "thing", always easily recognised, which is called the reflection process. It can be manifested in a variety of ways, sometimes blatantly, sometimes very subtly. Its recognition and the practice of using it can, in some instances, be very difficult.

I illustrate some of these manifestations in the fourth chapter, and the examples are taken from the work of the three groups, the Exeter workshop and the two London-based courses. These examples are taken from transcripts of tape-recordings of the seminars. It was the principal officers in Devon who first made the suggestion that we ought to try to formulate what we were doing in the workshop. The ideas should be more generally available. We felt this was just, but before being able to do this we needed the material in greater detail than our memories would allow. For a period of two years all the seminars were tape-recorded. The description of the cases and of the supervision is given in the supervisors' own words. I then quote some of the actual discussion to illustrate the way of working, how the group handled the presented material, the difficulties of sticking with this type of task, and where the group also acted out the reflection. But I have summarised much of the discussion in my own words. Like most group discussions, they were disjointed, repetitive, muddled, and, at times, dispirited and sunk in gloom. As they stand, and without accompanying description and a considerable amount of editing, they would be too painful and too unintelligible to read.

In the fifth chapter I illustrate the difference between a type of supervision which uses a theoretical model based on ideas of inter-action which I have described in this book and a type which is not, and I amplify a few points in the preceding text.

Having made the decision to try to write something on this subject, I was faced with a question which again increased my doubts. I could find no reference to the subject in the British social work literature. Were these ideas with which we had fumbled, and which we had tried to develop, quite unsubstantiated elsewhere? In my own parlance, "were we up the wall?" Could we just declare our ideas? It was with great relief that I discovered Searles describes the same process in writing of his psychiatric practice. It is he whom I mainly quote, and whose definitions I have used. But his work has led me to other references which indicate that we have not been completely wasting our time, although we have still not got very far in our thinking and we are still struggling to understand the phenomenon.

CHAPTER TWO

BASIC ASSUMPTIONS

The Involvement of the Worker

In the first chapter there is the assumption that it is appropriate for the worker to react to the client and to become involved, and that it is appropriate for the supervisor to react to the worker and to the work he is doing and describing. But this view is not held by all social workers, nor by all social work teachers, and certainly not by many people who advise on careers. It is still relatively common for intending social workers to be told that they should not take up the work if they feel they will get involved in, and affected by, the misery and trials and tribulations of the clients.

Much of the social work literature available in this country in the 1950s and early 1960s reinforced this view, although stating it more subtly and in more confused terms. Casework was mainly described as a principled activity. The worker should, for example, be accepting and non-judgemental.[1] There was philosophical discussion on what this meant, and whether it was the sinner or the sin which should be accepted.[2] Workers were advised to stretch out a long arm to save their drowning clients, but to be sure that they kept both feet on the bank.[3] "To be able to extend a helping hand to those in difficulty or distress requires, paradoxically enough, a capacity to respond warmly and sympathetically to them and their problems or to feel their unhappiness, while remaining at the same time sufficiently apart to avoid the risk of adding difficulties through undue emotional involvement."[4] This message is paralysing in two ways. It is difficult to imagine the state of getting close enough to clients to be able to help them talk about their fears and fantasies and at the same time remaining enough apart to be unaffected by those fears and by the actual behaviour of the client. And it assumes that the worker is of another species, unlike his clients and unlike the rest of mankind, non-introjecting, and always able to resist being pushed into a role, even by the most manipulative.

By the end of the 1960s these "rules of thumb" were being questioned and criticised by some writers.[5] In 1970, Jordan said, "The biggest weakness is that the game is formulated in such a way that it often seems as if only the social worker has aims and plans and things he is trying to do to the client. It fails to take account of the things the client is trying to do to him. It is like describing the game of cricket purely from the bowler's point of view, acknowledging that the batsman may do things that make it difficult to get him out (the client may have resistances against treatment) but failing to recognise that the batsman is aiming to make runs off the bowler."[6] In his book, *Client-Worker Transactions*, he more realistically described the live interchanges, at times defensive and not understood, at times understood, at times worked with and changed, that go on between clients and workers, allowing the worker to be human and to be subject to the same processes of interaction as his neighbours, influenced as well as influencing.

Casework, group work and community work are all based on the idea of influence, that the behaviour of one person will affect the behaviour of another person, either shifting or stabilising that mode, whether positively or negatively, either consciously or collusively. In continuing to use this basis in a *less one-sided fashion*, not forgetting that, "*You can exert no influence, if you are not susceptible to influence*,"[7] it is still necessary to consider what is the appropriate distance between client and worker in a truly interactive relationship. Relinquishing the idea of "sufficiently apart", what is sufficently close? In doing this we need to look at the whole question of balanced psychological distance.

Psychological Distance

The concept of psychological distance between people and the perennial problem of balanced distance are best illustrated by Schopenhauer's story of the porcupines, later quoted by Freud.[8]

> "A company of porcupines crowded themselves together one cold winter's day so as to profit by one another's warmth and so save themselves from being frozen to death. But soon they felt one another's quills, which induced them to separate again. And now, when the need for warmth brought them nearer together again, the second evil arose once more. So that they were driven backwards and forwards from one trouble to the other, until they had discovered a mean distance at which they could most tolerably exist."

The question facing caseworkers is how close they need to get to their clients to be able to help them and to allow them to profit from the worker's warmth. Most human beings "identify warmth with friendliness and coldness with hostility", and we can call a friendly person nourishing and a hostile person starving.[9] The closer the workers get the more likely they are to nourish and to influence their clients one way or another. But, at the same time, the closer they get the more likely they are to be affected themselves and to feel the quills. The more they care to listen to the depression of a client, the greater the weight of the sadness they will be left with, particularly if it touches on a similar sadness of their own. The more they are prepared to enter into a live transaction, less shielded by principle and more aware of their own reactions to the client, the more varied their behaviour will be, and the more knowledge they will have of how the behaviour of the client affects those with whom he comes into contact, including themselves.

There is no easy answer to this question. As in every relationship in life, whether personal, familial, leisure or work orientated, the comfortable distance has to be found by trial and error, as it was by the porcupines. It is different for different people in similar situations, and different for each person in many dissimilar situations. I think it is worth quoting Freud on this subject of distance:[10]

> "Let us keep before our eyes the nature of the emotional relations which hold between men in general. According to Schopenhauer's famous simile of the freezing porcupines, no one can tolerate a too intimate approach to his neighbours.
> "The evidence of psychoanalysis shows that almost every intimate emotional relationship between two people which lasts for some time— marriage, friendship, the relations between parents and children— leaves a sediment of feelings of aversion and hostility, which only escapes perception as a result of repression. This is less disguised in the common wrangles between business partners or in the grumbles of a subordinate at his superior. The same thing happens when men come together in larger units. Every time two families become connected by marriage, each of them thinks itself superior to or of better birth than the other. Of two neighbouring towns, each is the other's most jealous rival; every little canton looks down upon the other with contempt. Closely related races keep one another at arm's length; the South German cannot endure the North German, the Englishman casts every kind of aspersion upon the Scot, the Spaniard despises the Portuguese . . .
> "When this hostility is directed against people who are otherwise loved we describe it as ambivalence of feeling; and we explain the fact, in what is probably far too rational a manner, by means of numerous occasions for conflicts of interest which arise precisely in such intimate relations. In the undisguised antipathies and aversions which people feel towards strangers with whom they have to do we may recognise the expression of self-love—of narcissism. This self-love works for the preservation of the individual, and behaves as though the occurrence of any divergence from his own particular lines of development involved a criticism of them and a demand for their alteration. We do not know why such sensitiveness should have been directed to just these details of differentiation, but it is unmistakable that in this whole connection men give evidence of a readiness for hatred, an agressiveness, the course of which is unknown, and to which one is tempted to ascribe an elementary character."

But, if we accept this statement of a self-love and of a readiness for hatred which leaves even the most loving with a sediment of aversion and hostility, it is even more difficult to think in terms of a generalised appropriate distance. Some people's quills will be longer than those of others. I would not like to suggest that there is a correct distance or even a certain distance which the worker *should* maintain between his client and himself, nor that he can always be the arbiter of this distance, nor that the distance should remain the same throughout the transaction. I think one can only state and continually remind oneself about certain factors which will determine the different distances between different clients and different workers.

One of the agents in determining the distance is, of course, the client. Some will ask for warmth and closeness. Others, who feel they have suffered enough hurt in close relationships in the past, may insist on keeping their distance. The work with them may be about their coming closer to their spouses and children. And, if it feels safe enough, they may need to try this out with their worker first. Help in varying distance between themselves and others is sometimes required, so that they can exercise some choice in this, rather than compulsively perceiving everyone as having the same long, outstretched quills, poised at the ready to hurt.

Some clients may give a double message; their voices may bid the other to come closer, but their behaviour may ensure that he keeps his distance.

Other clients by their demands of closeness on too many people may finally drive them all away, including the caseworker. In marital work, when listening to couples talking about their relationship, it is apparent that some people have either a fantasy that they can literally get inside another, or an ideal of a state where there need be no distance and no difference in marriage. In these situations it is quite common to hear one partner always telling the other what the latter actually thinks and feels. When this type of couple comes for help at a point of crisis which they can no longer tolerate on their own, one partner is often in a state of collapse or depression and the other is frantically seeking an alternative relationship or relationships (on the principle of safety in numbers) as a means of retreat from the claustrophobia to which he has been a contributor. The lack of "breathing space" in this type of relationship is a characteristic which curtails the greater and more varied expression of individual personality and the potential creativity of the two persons, both separately within the partnership, and together.

The attempt of a parent to take over the personality of a child, determining his every thought, decision and action throughout his formative years, can result in a child putting up a false screen to protect his true self from such bombardment and intrusion; a variety of symptoms and obsessions, which then determine him as a patient in his own right (particularly when their continued maintenance becomes more difficult and they become more extreme in their expression), surround and shield the vital part of himself.[11] His false self may demand and react to excessive closeness, which is what he has been used to, but his true self may have to be kept particularly distant and out of other people's reach. In his relationship with a caseworker, he will probably veer dramatically from attempts to get close to attempts to keep himself safe, particularly until he dares to start to trust the worker's ability not to over-intrude.*

Quite apart from many other factors in the client's situation which may affect the distance he needs from the worker, the other agents in the determination of distance are the worker and his setting. Sometimes the setting precludes ways of working which allow closeness; lack of privacy for interviews, lack of time, lack of support, and a majority of tasks of a less personal nature to which priority has to be given. (But it must be remembered that elements in the organisational structure are often developed by its members in the struggle against the anxiety raised by the task. "An important aspect of such socially structured defence mechanisms is an attempt by individuals to externalise and give substance in objective reality to their characteristic psychic defence mechanisms."[15] These structured defences help individual workers avoid the experiences of anxiety, guilt, doubt and uncertainty, but at the same time may raise secondary anxieties and deprive them of some satisfactions. Menzies emphasises that the service itself does not operate defences. "Defences are, and can be, operated only by individuals." Membership of an organisation "necessitates an adequate degree of matching between individual and social defence systems."[16])

It is probably true to say that if a worker is personally very uncomfortable in the distance which is generally made possible by the nature of the tasks, priorities, and structure of the agency, and its institutionalised defence system, he will leave and find something more to his liking. But most social work departments do allow some leeway in which the worker can determine for himself how close or how distant he tries to be with his clients. And for his own reasons he will vary from his colleagues, and, when they allow him to do so, with different clients, in the distance with which he is most comfortable when working. In fact he and the client will probably drive each other backwards and forwards from one distance to another until they discover the mean at which they can most tolerably exist together.

During this process with a variety of clients the worker will, if he gives some thought to it, discover what is his own norm and at what point he is most comfortable in a working situation. It is then much

---

* "Avoiders" and "clingers" have been classified and described by Freud (the anaclitic and the narcissistic),[12] Fenichel (the phobic and the counter-phobic),[13] and Balint (the philobat and the ocnophil).[14] The latter has also related his theory of the primitive attitudes underlying the overt behaviour to treatment considerations.

more possible for him to look at whether he needs to extend or to lessen his distance with some clients to be able to give them more appropriate help and to start to consider when and why he might find this difficult. But, perhaps more important, as he gets to know his own norm, if instead of attempting to stick rigidly to this stance, he allows himself to be involved in a more dynamic way, he will have useful diagnostic information about the client when he perceives himself off his more usual stance—either pushed away or beckoned and getting closer. His own reaction will be a useful indicator and give him direct information of how the client distances himself from other people. The further the worker is pushed or pulled, the more he will know about the strength of the client's disturbance in inappropriately retreating from, or attempting to get close to, the other.

When considering the particular question of distance, it is useful for the worker to ask at the end of the interview, "How close or how distant was I, and how much did the client determine this?" And perhaps an even more important question is, "What did this client make me feel like?" But this brings us back to the original assumption of the need to be involved in a live and reacting way to the client. It is impossible to know what a client makes you feel like, if you do not lay yourself open to feelings that he may arouse. But is this a too painful and disorientating way of working over any length of time? If workers are reacting to a number of clients and feeling their own feelings and at times those of their clients which are projected into them, will they be under too much of a strain within a few months? Presumably the idea of a fixed distance, sufficiently apart, determined by principle or by a soulless methodology, unenlivened by reaction, was promoted to protect the worker.

I do not think it is helpful to deny that there is considerable stress in the work, but I believe, rather than protection and distancing from the stress, it is more helpful to the client and to the worker to think in terms of support in handling it in both a tighter and a freer way. The notion of boundaries is less negatively defensive than "sufficient distance" and more positively helpful both to the client and to the worker, allowing more freedom of manoeuvre within the framework.

Boundaries

The previous section could be summed up by saying that one of life's psychological problems for every individual is in finding, by trial and error, comfortable and satisfying distance from other people in different relationships, warm enough and not too prickly; a handling of the basic conflict between the need for warmth and the need not to be hurt by the defending and narcissistic manoeuvres of oneself and other people. In this section we could say that another of life's problems is knowing about our own boundary, the thickness or the thinness of our "psycho-logical skin", and what we can hold for ourselves within that boundary, including the basic conflict between self expression and self control.

It appears to be true that there can be very little real freedom experienced without this freedom being defined by its outer limits. Perhaps it is the fear of a chaos which is expected to occur, or has previously occurred, in infancy or adult life, when limits are, or have been, or are perceived to have been, non-existent or unknown. Some people can relatively easily place their own limits and choose where they put the boundary round their freedom, but many of us find this difficult to handle in some areas of our lives and need the constraint to be external. Probably the majority of people are a mixture of strengths and weaknesses, holding their own boundary in respect of some things and not of others. Rules, regulations, rituals and formalised roles and structures are the means we use to help ourselves and others in keeping boundaries. The lesser the internal ability for boundary keeping, whether this is actually exercised or not, the more the external con-straints are necessary. Before discussing some external constraints or boundary placing round the actual casework situation, it is necessary to say a little more about the concept of the individual having a definite boundary which is recognisable to himself and to others. This is relevant to both clients and workers. Some will have thick skins, some will have thin.

The idea of a thick or a thin skin as an effective or ineffective bound-ary, both physically and psychologically, is used in everyday speech. People refer to their light and tender skin which easily burns in the sun. And sunstroke can penetrate the skin and set up other internal symptoms. The expression "thick-skinned" is often used derogatively to describe the insensitive. And in medical and psychiatric language, skin complaints have been described as boundary or barrier diseases.

Much of the dynamic psychological literature on interactive processes observes the lack of distinct psychological boundaries between people and the amount of unconscious, as well as conscious, communication between them. A simple example is that of hysteria, a catching phenom-enon, which can be easily seen and experienced in a large crowd. Psychoanalysts have paid attention to what happens to the parts of the self which the individual cannot know about, either repressing or disowning them and putting them outside the self. In the Institute of Marital Studies we have made use of the psychoanalytic concepts of projection, introjection, and projective identification in attempting to understand patterns of interaction, particularly prominent in marriage, in which both partners, having chosen the other as their particular object of attachment, are both the subject and the object in the treat-ment together.

It is very noticeable in the most uncomfortable of marriages that not only are the partners unable to find a little more distance between themselvés, but there is such a lack of boundary round each of them that it is very difficult to know who is responsible for what in the tangle of arguments and abuse and recriminations in joint interviews. The workers can become as confused as the clients, and the argument can get into their relationship in their attempts to try to understand what is happening. And in these situations it is often apparent that the couple have an unconscious but vested interest in together keeping the workers as confused as themselves. It is also noticeable that the tighter and more rigid the system of mutual defence, the less the couple can tolerate any prospect of separation; it is never even mentioned as a possibility.

In a recent pilot and retrospective follow-up study,[17] through which we wanted to sensitize ourselves to how clients had viewed the type of treatment offered in the Institute, many of these clients commented on what we came to call the "enmeshment" of their relationship. The work seemed to have been untangling the enmeshment and finding out who they themselves were. One couple, commenting that this type of relationship had existed between them and their friends as well, and that they were as much involved in the similar troubles of these friends as they were in their own, said that when they got themselves into their own skins they could agree to separate, which meant they could then agree to remain married. Then they no longer needed the workers, "Thank you very much". Each of them was enough in their own skin to recognise the difference of the other, to start to relate more appropriately to that difference, and to get on with the business of being married on their own.

This does not mean that people who are relatively mentally healthy (knowing about their own individuality and that of others, with its strengths and weaknesses, aware of and able to hold and tolerate a degree of conflict within themselves and between them and other people in a more benign and less mutually destructive way) have such thick skins that they are not affected by the other, or that they cease to use the whole range of psychic defences against strong feelings— their own and those of others. It does mean, however, that they can use these defences more moderately, more flexibly, and with less compulsion. It does mean that their psychological skin is firm enough to hold and know about many of their own feelings and often—not always —to be able to distinguish what belongs to them and what belongs to other people. And, although they may often use words and actions to express their feelings spontaneously, it does mean that tension from unrecognised feelings is not discharged regardlessly and endlessly by compulsive behaviour which, in the jargon, we call "acting-out".

This phrase is usually applied to clients, and has been defined as "a replacement activity".[18] The term, borrowed from psychoanalysis, is "used to cover the acting of unconscious experience in an inappropriate setting". On many occasions, however, it can be applied to workers; many disturbed and immature people discharge tension not by their own acting-out, but by manipulating others, including social workers, to do it for them. Again, relative maturity does not mean never acting-out. Technically, we can say it is not acting-out when we are aware of the feeling we are expressing, however socially undesirable the act may be. But in casework there are many occasions when we act-out for our clients, and literally so, when we are not aware that we are doing it. This is sometimes considered to be, if not a sin, at least unprofessional, but in the next section, which is about working with the transference of feeling, I shall suggest that the worker sometimes needs to participate in the relationship to the extent of being prepared to act-out in order to *know* about the feelings the client cannot hold for himself.

He certainly needs to be able to accept a projection from the client before he can know what the client is projecting. His psychological skin needs to be sensitive enough to pick up some of the psychic difficulties of his client, but it needs to be firm enough round his own being to be able to distinguish between what belongs to him and what is, in fact, some feeling he has introjected from the client. This was illustrated in the introduction. Both *The Wasp* and *The Scribe* depicted the workers and the supervisors acting-out some unknown feelings for the clients. By seeing their actions in this light and then looking at what might be the feelings behind these actions, they were helped to be more conscious of their reaction, less compelled by, but a little bit more in touch with, the clients' strength of feeling, and then more effective in the work.

However aware the worker is of his own psychological boundary, many of his clients will not respect this, nor be aware of their own. They will be unable to use or experiment with the potential freedom he offers them to explore their difficulties, if this freedom is not tightly defined and limited by a known external boundary. And the worker, if he is going to use himself more fully in this situation, will also need this boundary.

Time is one obvious boundary. Most workers know for themselves that if they let a highly-charged interview last several hours, they are fit for very little next day. And the client, if he is to use the time more effectively, needs to know in advance how much he can have of the worker's time, whether it is fifteen, thirty or sixty minutes. The less sense of time he himself has, or the more he is threatened by the nature of the work, the more he will need to have this boundary made for him. Regularity of time is another aspect of keeping a boundary, particularly with clients who for the present find it difficult to hold either their depression or their anxiety on their own. If they know when relief is coming, they are less likely to produce a crisis in the meantime.

Regularity of place is another boundary keeper, whether it is the client's own home or an interviewing room in the office. It helps to define the situation and helps to keep it safe. It is easy to under-estimate how much very disturbed clients, rocketing backwards and forwards with their emotions, depend on the familiarity and safeness of the concrete. And the increasingly known becomes increasingly safe. I have been amazed when some clients have complained bitterly that my room had just been repainted. It was not the same in its pristine state. They hated it, and it made them feel very peculiar. One very disturbed IMS client was seen regularly in the home of his worker. In the follow-up study he referred to this as not being clinical enough, and it was clear that he would have felt his madness better contained in a more institutional building.

Again, there are no hard and fast rules as to what clients can or cannot tolerate, and as to the boundaries needed round the work to enable clients and workers to use the relationship more effectively. Certainly the worker will be emotionally freer and do better work if he is comfortable within the setting and knows where the boundaries are. Different clients can use different situations and tolerate varying degrees of change. But perhaps it is important to remember that the more disturbed the client, the less he is in his own skin, and the more he psychologically bombards the worker, the tighter the external boundary round the working situation needs to be.

In this and the last section I have mentioned some basic assumptions which are simple and unsophisticated—life, warmth and closeness, and therefore at times discomfort from narcissistic quills, and the support in handling this afforded by better boundary-keeping rather than protection from it by a cool, fixed and remote distance. And I have done this because the rest of the chapter would be meaningless if there was confusion in the text as to whether it was appropriate to get involved with the client. Use of the reflection process necessitates a willingness to get involved and the main thesis of this book rests on the assumption, as Guntrip said in a lecture at the Tavistock Centre in 1973, "that it is the personal relationship which is therapeutic, not something called the 'technique of interpretation' ".[19] He believes that "the real therapist is born, not trained, but that he knows how to make the best use of training when he gets it." And I am anticipating the next section when I quote Racker, who states, "It should also be remembered how much importance Freud assigned to the positive transference in the process of regaining health. . . . In this context Freud speaks of the 'boiling heat (*Siedehitze*) of the transference', and according to my experience such temperatures can only be achieved if the worker also contributes sufficient heat—sufficient positive counter-transference made real through his work . . ."[20]

The reflection process is part of the countertransference.

Transference and Countertransference

One of Freud's most important discoveries was that of transference. When he moved from the hypnotic method to that of free association, interpreting repressed feelings, impulses and resistances of his patients, he found that after a period of collaboration, they seemed to lose interest in the past and turned towards the present, an immediate present concerning Freud himself. When the investigation reached a particularly sensitive point, the patient, instead of remembering, reproduced a feeling and a reaction from that past situation and directed it towards the therapist. The feelings in relation to the therapist were a displaced repetition of older ones. Impulses and feelings were trans-ferred. In his definition, "re-impressions and reproductions of the emo-tions and phantasies . . . , characterised by the replacement of a former person by the physician",[21] he does not make explicit the irrationality of this, although this is generally accepted.

A more recent definition of transference is: "the experiencing of feelings, drives, attitudes, fantasies and defences towards a person in the present which do not befit that person but are a repetition of reactions originating in regard to significant persons of early childhood, unconsciously displaced on to figures in the present."[22] One of the definitions I like best, however, is that of Jung, given in a lecture at the Tavistock Clinic in 1935: " an awkward hanging on, an adhesive sort of relationship".[23] More seriously, he had previously defined it as consisting of "a number of projections which act as a substitute for a real psychological relationship" due to the client's habitual failure to adapt to the actuality of the other.[24] He also made the point that the projections formed an emotional link, or a bridge, because he said, emotions are not detachable, have physical manifestations and are deeply rooted in the body.[25] The transference relationship, therefore, is an extremely useful way of getting in touch for people who find it difficult to make contact in a more realistic way. It is a substitute for a "true" relationship—I-Thou. Instead of being influenced by the actuality of the other, with the flexibility which that affords, it is dominated by the situation—I-It—of the inner world.

This way of relating is not, of course, confined to therapeutic situa-tions. Freud's discovery that it happened in therapeutic relationships made it possible to see more clearly its manifestations in other rela-tionships. We do not enter any new situation with a clean slate of perception and react accordingly. Our expectation, based on our previous experience and way of handling that experience, colours our perception of the new, of the way we react and the way we will force other people to react to us. "The ego brings something of its own towards the object to be perceived."[26] As experiments by social psychologists have shown, our generally faulty perception, very much coloured by our previous experience, is at its most faulty at the two extremes—with the very unfamiliar and with the most familiar.[27] Spouses are often as much misperceived as people of another race and colour. (It is because the transference of feeling in marriage is more pronounced than in many other less familiar relationships that work with marriages has proved to be a useful learning experience for social workers; the consistent projections and introjections are often less subtle and can be more readily seen in a marital relationship than in many others[28]).

Bearing in mind that our perceptions are "an amalgam of a reaction to a 'real' person, out there, plus the projection upon him of the perceiver's internal complexes . . . I suggest," says Gordon, "that we designate it as a 'true' relationship when awareness of the 'other' is formed, predominantly, by the facts of the real person out there, while in a transference relationship the pressures of the internal needs create distortions which do violence to the existence and to the wholeness of that other person."[29]

The phenomenon of transference at first seemed a disturbing discovery, but soon became valued as presenting an opportunity for misperceptions to be corrected. A new experience could be offered in which the fantasy could be tested against the present reality. This, in its turn, could direct future perception of other situations and relationships. On this basis, it is very important for the client to perceive a live worker who reacts.

Understanding something about transference relationships does not mean that the social worker always needs to interpret this to the client. In many situations an interpretation is quite inappropriate and a lot of good casework is done when the transference is never actually mentioned. But it is probably helpful to the worker to know quite clearly in his own mind when a client is displaying a strong transference reaction, and when he is not. If he fails to do this, he will grossly underestimate the reactions, feelings and fantasies of those clients who are operating on this basis.

A strong transference relationship is characterised by a distorted perception of the stimulus, an over-extended, or inappropriate, or untimely, and often repetitive reaction, provoked by the underlying need to make the present relationship fit into the psychodynamic structure of a previous one. It is not a transference reaction if the client reacts solely to the present stimulus, either the warmth or niceness of the worker, or the coldness, unreliability, lateness, or unconscious hostility of the worker. (In the last instance, he is responding to subliminal clues.)

It is also important to remember that, although strong transference reactions are related to the most important figures, such as mothers and fathers and siblings, in very early experiences when the client was most vulnerable and dependent, it is the detail, and not the fact, which is important. It is of little help to know that a client is projecting feelings that he had for his mother on to the worker; what is important and useful to know is the type of feeling and the way this distorts the reaction in the present—that a particular feeling is inappropriately enacted, or cannot be held and is projected into the worker or some other person who could be taken to represent the original figure.

Classically, countertransference was seen to be only the reverse of transference—the worker's, not the client's, transference. Freud first recognised this in 1910, mainly in terms of its dangers.[30] For many years, the worker's having strong feelings about his client was held most suspect. But, after a long silence, the concept was widened and enriched by several writers who perceived the countertransference as a function of the transference of the client.[31] The reaction of the worker to the client's transference need not be condemned, but could be noticed and used for increasing the understanding of the client's behaviour.[32] Winnicott used the term, "the objective countertransference", meaning "the worker's love and hate reaction to the actual personality and behaviour of the patient . . ."[33] Countertransference came to be seen as an "innate and inevitable ingredient"[34] of a therapeutic relationship.

In this monograph I am concerned with these three different aspects of countertransference:—

an innate and inevitable ingredient,

which is sometimes a conscious reaction to the observed behaviour of the client, or which is sometimes an unconscious reaction to the felt and not consciously understood behaviour of the client,

and which can be used for increasing understanding of the client.

And with reference to Searles, I am also concerned with a fourth aspect:—

the resolution by the worker of the countertransference as one of the main ingredients of casework which enables the client to resolve and relinquish the transference.[35]

If the worker, as part of his work, has to resolve his countertransference, he must, therefore, have a countertransference to resolve. He must be well in the situation. Countertransference ceases to have a solely negative connotation.

Obviously the phenomenon described in the classical definition can occur and cannot be ignored. But I find it easier to distinguish this as the transference of the worker and to refer to it as such. Countertransference I define, for the purpose of this monograph, as *the reaction to the transference*. The two are, of course, connected. The worker's perception, like that of any other person, will be partially pre-determined by his earlier experiences and perceptions of those experiences. He can react only from what is within him already, and his capacity to react consciously will depend on the degree to which he is conscious of himself; what he picks up from the client unconsciously, he will react to unconsciously. I will be coming back to the subject of the transference of the worker and the connection between the transference and the countertransference in the final chapter.

In this section I am concerned with the use of the countertransference, as I defined it in the above paragraph. I expect all workers can remember very strong countertransference feelings in particular pieces of work. I remember one client with whom I had a terrible tendency to go to sleep. It happened week after week. Although I knew I did not have this tendency with my other clients, and never had had it, I did wonder whether the combination of my middle age and a two o'clock appointment determined this. But it happened just the same one week when the appointment was altered to eleven o'clock. It was only with the help of my supervisor that I was able to see the connection between the psychic bombardment she delivered on me and what she had told me about her history. It was interesting that the sibling whom she used to bombard in a more physical way, in an expression of mixed love and hate, did not do well at school, nor in her career, just as I was not doing very well as a therapist.

In one initial consultation a client complained of his wife's lack of ability to enjoy herself with him and of her school ma'am attitude. But, as his inappropriate and discordant laughter rocked him and the chair he was sitting in while he told me of much sadness and destructive behaviour, I felt my face become stonier and stonier and my own attitude more that of the ma'am. When I commented on my reaction and said that I could not laugh about some of the things he had told me and felt myself becoming like his description of his wife, he replied that his secretary had also commented the previous week about his facetious laughter. When, perhaps, I can laugh spontaneously with this client, I will know he is getting better and is more in touch with what he is feeling and doing.

Once the members of the workshop at Exeter complained of the inhumanity of my colleague and myself after we had presented a case and had described the clients as unlikeable. In fact I felt that the client's sneer had been the most dislikeable I had ever met. I remember saying, "Although, now I come to think of it, I don't know what shame really is, never in my life have I met such a dislikeable lack of shame." This has to be set against the knowledge that on the whole I do not dislike my clients, so that the important question became why did this couple have to make themselves so dislikeable to the workers, and therefore, presumably, to other people. It is difficult to imagine that people would do this on purpose. This we had consciously perceived, but, in our presentation, we unconsciously continued to react to many other facets of their behaviour, and the group was able to help us pick up how split we had become. Despite our supposed "joint" presentation, we had become on non-speaking and non-listening terms with each other and were both relating to and discussing with the group quite independently and without reference to the other. This is a common phenomenon in casework discussion groups when the split in the case gets into the group, but in this instance it was particularly apparent.

Many clients who come for help have very dislikeable traits in their character and one of the indications that they are getting better is that they become more likeable.

In describing why it is important to react to the client I can think of no better example than that given by Searles in his paper, "Oedipal Love and the Countertransference".[36] Generally he is promoting the idea that it is even more important to react to the schizophrenic client than any other, just because that type of client has a poorly established contact with reality, and because his "abysmally low self-esteem is nourished by whatever emotional response . . ." he is "able to arouse in his therapist." But in talking about helping a child to establish a good contact with reality, he refers to his feelings for his own daughter.

"Not only my work with patients but also my experience as a husband and a parent have convinced me of the validity of the concepts I am offering here. Towards my daughter, now eight years of age, I have experienced innumerable fantasies and feelings of a romantic-love kind, thoroughly complementary to the romantically adoring, seductive behaviour which she has shown towards her father sometimes ever since she was about two or three years of age. I used at times to feel somewhat worried when she would play the supremely confident coquette with me and I would feel enthralled by her charms; but then I came to the conviction, some time ago, that such moments of relatedness could only be nourishing for her developing personality as well as delightful to me. If a little girl cannot feel herself able to win the heart of her father, her own father who has known her so well and for so long, and is tied to her by mutual blood-ties, I reasoned, then how can the young woman who comes later have any deep confidence in the power of her womanliness. "And I have had every impression, similarly, that the oedipal desires of my son, now eleven years of age, have found a similarly lively and whole-hearted feeling-response in my wife; and I am equally convinced that their deeply fond, openly evidenced mutual attraction is good for my son as well as enriching to my wife. To me it makes sense that the more a woman loves her husband, the more she will love, similarly, the lad who is, to at least a considerable degree, the younger edition of the man she loved enough to marry."

In continuing to speak of healthy relationships between children and parents, he emphasises the resolution of the oedipal strivings, not just by identification with the forbidding rival parent, but through the ego strengthening experience of the reciprocation by the loved parent and then the renunciation by the latter with a real accompanying sense of loss. This is made in deference to reality, including the taboo maintained by the rival parent, but also because of the love between the parents to which the child owes his existence. He supports this view by his experience of people in treatment whose ego growth, he found, was impaired by the parent's denial of his own feelings, which were then unwittingly acted-out in unduly seductive behaviour only to be excessively counteracted by punishment of the "unlovable", "undesirable" child. And in talking about his work with these patients, he says,

"I have grown successively less troubled at finding such responses (i.e. *intense feelings*) in myself, less constrained to conceal these from the patient, and increasingly convinced that they augur well rather than ill for the outcome of our relationship, and that the patient's self-esteem benefits greatly from his sensing that he is capable of arousing such responses in the analyst. I have come to believe that there is a direct correlation between, on the one hand, the *affective intensity* with which the analyst experiences an awareness of such feelings—and of the unrealizability of such feelings—in himself towards the patient, and, on the other hand, the depth of maturation which the patient achieves. . . . and the patient, when he or she has achieved sufficient ability to recognise and accept the analyst as a real person, will sense that the analyst has such feelings and that he is able to cope safely with them."

Searles is speaking in this paper of analytic treatment and of the use of his reaction to oedipal and sexual feelings of patients. But the points he makes so vividly in relation to his children and to his patients and to love reactions are valid and relevant for caseworkers dealing with this phenomenon and with a variety of other countertransference feelings. Perhaps one of the most important statements he makes about the need to have and then to handle the reaction is that the worker "has such feelings and that he is able to cope safely with them".

In *True and False Experience*[37] Lomas, like Searles and Guntrip, has emphasised the importance of a live reaction, and the handling of that reaction, as one of the most important parts of therapy. He says. ". . . I have become increasingly less inclined to view the psychotherapeutic process as a medical or scientific endeavour. It is, I believe, less a matter of applying a technique than forming a relationship, less an attempt to treat a sick person than to find one's way through the false ways in which a person may live, and help him to experience life more truly. . . . If its aim is to reveal the patient's capacity to experience life in a real way, then one can only expect this to happen if the therapist himself acts in the encounter as a real person; true experience has little chance of emerging in a false setting."

He talks of workers' fears of too deep an emotional involvement, the fear of being unscientific, of shyness and modesty in exposing warmth, realism and honesty as part of their therapeutic endeavour. He asks why these qualities, expressed by friends and not only by therapists, are the effective agents of psychotherapy. He suggests two reasons why therapists are sometimes more successful than friends and relatives, not just because of their technical know-how, which hopefully can become part of themselves rather than a studied, technical, scientific pose; firstly, he says, the therapist is "placed in a position calculated to evoke the best in him"; and secondly, he has previous "experience in treating sick people", experience of "the way in which human anguish manifests itself and the sort of response that is needed to help".

Lomas supports the view that much therapy requires a holding of the patient so that he can give up "his pretence of functioning adequately and can explore, imagine and develop rather in the way in which a baby can grow in the presence of a mother who supports but does not unduly impinge." What he does not emphasise as explicitly as Searles, is the relinquishment of the countertransference—that the success of any treatment, or any part of treatment, depends on the worker's resolution of the countertransference, which he must have had in order to have something to relinquish. As Searles so clearly explained after his description of his feelings for his daughter, it is the parent's relinquishment of the child and his own sense of loss which helps to strengthen the child's ego and sense of identity.

The examples given by Searles and Lomas of their own work mainly illustrate their overcoming of their own defences in going into a loving countertransference and their toleration of their own loving and sexual feelings. And certainly many social workers, like many psychotherapists, have difficulty in feeling safe enough to be able to do this. But we are also concerned with less loving countertransference reactions— reactions to the unpleasant facets of our clients' behaviour, and unconscious reactions to facets of the clients' behaviour which we do not understand. Students and young workers are particularly vulnerable to the latter. And as teachers we are often concerned with this. It can be argued that clients should be protected from these reactions, and that students should be advised to keep their distance. I suggest the opposite, however, and that for diagnostic reasons and as part of the helping process, the worker (whether he is a formal student or not), hopefully ever learning, should be encouraged to get closer. I have three reasons.

Firstly, it takes more skill to handle the situation and to hold the client when psychologically distant. A worker can be affected by his client's strongest projections irrespective of a conscious desire to remain uninfluenced by him. Emotional interaction operates at numerous levels and the worker can protect himself from things that are conscious, but not from those that are unconscious. Psychological distance does not protect him. In fact it increases the negative transference. He is even more exposed to the strongest negative projections which remain unmitigated by the ambivalence and the mixture of both positive and negative feelings that are picked up and used in a warmer and closer relationship. Consciously increasing the psychological distance to get the negative transference more clearly enacted and felt by worker and client is a justifiable technique (used by many analysts) for someone who knows what they are doing and why they are doing it, and who can then handle and interpret it therapeutically. Psychological distance determined on the principle of safety and lack of involvement, with a corresponding lack of recognition of the increased exposure to only the most powerful projections, "has the paradoxical effect of getting the worker unknowingly more deeply involved with the client's most negative features."[38] His conscious decision not to be involved will further blunt his capacity to look at the collusive nature of his behaviour. Action supposedly based on an "objective" decision, because of the distance from which it has been made, is often a horrifyingly accurate reflection and confirmation of the client's worst fears. An example of this is the situation of a very disturbed client who feels he is so bad, or so mad, that only being "put away" will do. This type of client invariably interprets the worker's coolness and distance as a need to keep away from him. It confirms his worst fears of how damaging he is to people. Even more uncomfortable than he was before, he contains the feeling even less well and therefore projects it even more strongly. The worker suddenly finds himself setting things in motion to get the order made for compulsory confinement which the client, having projected the feeling, resists with all his might.

Secondly, in less extreme situations, very little therapy is achieved on an uninvolved or distant basis, intellectual as that must be. An interpretation which is made without reference to what is happening in the present may give some insight, but rarely seems to affect actual behaviour. An interpretation eventually made, or even better a shared understanding between two people with both of them contributing, about some piece of interaction which has been acted and felt by both of them in the present or recent past, is what effects change. There is then, it seems, a real inner knowing about what has been interpreted. I know from my own experience how very bored I have been, and how little I have been able to learn, in a group situation in which some members, very experienced in T-group type phenomena, have interpreted everything before it happened—or at least happened for me. I was left feeling very dull and slow. I did not know what they were talking about, when I had not felt it nor seen it with my own eyes, and did not know it in my own immediate experience. I often am very slow on the up-take, but so are many clients. Many things need to be lived through in the present situation, before they can be meaningfully perceived and then corrected.

Thirdly, I do not think clients are helped in acquiring a better sense of reality if the worker is too superior a being — one who believes that he does not collude at times, that he cannot or should not be influenced, and that he sometimes does not walk into traps which the clients set for him. A worker who has walked into a trap and can then do something about it—can resolve something, can relinquish some aspect of his behaviour—is not only providing a more realistic model, but gives the client hope that he can do likewise. As Lomas said, "Limitation of growth occurs, I believe, whenever the parent 'keeps the child in his place' . . . that is to say, whenever the parent conceives of the child as essentially different from himself." Omnipotence is probably the most disastrous characteristic for any social worker, and too much reliance on technique, as opposed to response and then understanding what the response is about, fosters omnipotence.

I remember often saying, when I worked as a tutor for the social work course at Exeter, that I did not mind how involved the students became. I and their supervisors could attempt to pull them back. But I felt there was no starting point for training if they could not go into a situation enough to react to it. I do not think I really knew what I was saying, but I was expressing a way of working. By encouraging them to go in and then pulling them back, I was, in more sophisticated language, helping them to resolve the countertransference. Like many tutors and supervisors, I was often amazed that students did so well with many of their clients—ones with whom previous and experienced workers had failed. I often attributed this to the students' need to be successful, but perhaps it was also to do with their walking into the situation with both feet, often with a rather clumsy jump, before getting out of it. Dr Jean Packman, commenting on the students' dissertations, has often exclaimed at their honesty; when describing some of their work, they admitted to many of the crassest things they had said to their clients and subsequently knocked themselves on the head for doing it and put it right.

The rest of this monograph is about the countertransference to the client's behaviour and where this is so pervasive and un-understood that it is reflected in the supervision process. Sometimes the supervisor reacts collusively as well. These reactions are not to the detriment of the worker or the supervisor. By allowing themselves to be influenced, by reacting, and by exposing their reaction to the other, they are able to learn what is happening with the client, which then gives them a chance of overcoming their part in the difficulty. The worker is then perceived by the client as a creature not so different from himself, actually doing something about the difficulty which they have been in together and in which they have both been human beings. Perhaps it is this, alongside the more practised understanding of the anguish, and the times when the worker does not collude, that really affects the course of any helping process.

CHAPTER THREE

THE REFLECTION PROCESS

To reflect is "to show the image".[1] The reflection process is an image of the countertransference and of the transference as I defined these terms for use in this monograph in the last chapter—the countertransference being the response to the client's transference which itself is characterised by an inappropriate reaction and a need to make the present relationship fit into the psycho-dynamic structure of a previous relationship.

When the worker consciously perceives and understands what the client is trying to do, he can choose either to refuse to respond, or to respond, knowing what he himself is doing. Whichever way he reacts he can also choose whether to interpret his and the client's interaction or not. He is master of his own response and behaviour.

However, when he does not consciously know what the client is asking of him or what the client is trying to defend against, his response will have less range; it may be one of confusion or of fright or of distancing. Whether he aims to be involved or not, he will unconsciously react to the exaggerated behaviour of the client, or, as we often say, he will collude. I think it is true to say that the more the client's behaviour is, in the present situation, over-extended from the current stimulus, ie. pathological, and the more that behaviour is not consciously understood, the greater the collusive reaction of the worker is likely to be. So, although it is difficult to say precisely by what mechanism the reflection process occurs, it is not surprising that the greater the disturbance of the client, and the greater the collusive reaction of the worker in the actual situation, the less the worker will be able to relinquish his reaction, particularly when he tries to describe or re-live the interview with his supervisor.

One way of describing is to mimic, particularly for vividness, and particularly if we cannot find adequate words to portray the phenomenon. We often think of mimicry as an amusing social skill, admiring those who can consciously do it with wit and humour. Unconsciously we all mimic, probably more than we realise, continually picking up ways and attitudes from other people without giving them conscious thought. Unless this is done continuously and wholesale without an eventual selective process, it does not appear to be harmful. When watching children at domestic and re-enactive play, one can observe the elements of mimicry—mimicry of parents, teachers, shopkeepers, doctors and nurses. Children play hardest at games and repeat those games most often when they are trying to come to terms with some experience which is painful, or are trying to master the anxiety aroused. It does not seem extraordinary that students—"children at social work"—do this more often than experienced workers. It may be that identification as a means of coming to terms with some phenomenon is one of the most usual and basic forms of psychic management, and may be reverted to more strenuously for a period in a learning situation —whether learning about a trade or whether learning about life— in attempting to deal with any new experience. It is when the identification is blind and without discrimination that it remains false to the personality.

And it is the false behaviour, out of character with the worker's personality and previous experience, which reveals the reflection process in casework supervision. It is literally a reflection, or a mimicry, of one situation in a related and adjacent situation. It is a transference —a need to make the present relationship fit into the psycho-dynamic structure of a previous one—but for clarity it is easier to limit the term "transference" to what is carried into the present from the historical past, and use the term "reflection" for what is carried over from the immediate past with the client into the adjacent situation of supervision.

Because what is reflected is over-determined, on the part both of the client and of the worker, and therefore has considerable power behind it, it is not difficult for the supervisor to join in the collusive process and in his turn react accordingly without seeing what he is doing. He may react with or against the transference, as the worker may have done in the interview.

I think it is necessary to distinguish whether the countertransference in the work and then in the supervision is "for" (an inappropriate going-along-with), or "against" (an antagonism), or a confused mixture of the two. There are several possibilities in the working situation and the permutation is increased with the additional figure in the supervision.

One way of its working—and perhaps the simplest to see, although not all that common—is that of straight identification. The client seduces or manipulates the worker into a way of thinking, feeling and acting like him; the worker loses his boundary and in the supervision enacts the client's behaviour, which has become indistinguishable from his own. The supervisor can fail to notice the change in the worker's behaviour, and can either also identify, or he can react against his behaviour, but just as defensively and as collusively. Or he can pick up the reflection, the falseness to the worker, and look at the power this client has to influence people and his need to get them close to him, even to the point of making them the same as himself, or even, metaphorically, of getting inside them.

Another manifestation, subtler but much more common, is that of the worker not necessarily having been openly seduced in the interview, but so confused as to what is going on that he portrays aspects of the client's behaviour to the supervisor. In his attempt to describe what he cannot put into words, he unconsciously mimics. The supervisor may be left as confused as the worker and, although he may have a wider range of reaction than the younger worker, his reaction is likely to be of the same order as that of the worker in the actual interview, in that it portrays a defence against the insecurity of not knowing and of not understanding. He may, therefore, react like a relative of the client. This was apparent in the two examples given in the Introduction. In *The Wasp*, the student mimicked the mother over and beyond her own defence which gave the supervisor a feeling that she was impenetrable. The son could only get the mother to respond after the third and very serious offence, and the supervisor could only get the student to respond by excessive stinging. In *The Scribe*, the child could only put his feelings onto paper, and in the supervision, when the student described his difficulties with that mother and of the tea-party atmosphere which she attempted to set up, it was the supervisor who had to cut through the muddling facade and attempt to give form on paper to what lay behind it.

In social work there are often two or more clients—sometimes a whole family. In these two illustrations there were two active clients at the time in each case. In these situations it is likely that if the worker is portraying some aspects of the behaviour of one of them, the supervisor will be forced into the role of the other.

A third manifestation is when the client attempts to make the worker feel what it was like to be him. It is relatively common for a very disturbed client to enact some hated piece of behaviour of one of his parents, so that the worker really knows what he had to endure. And when this is reflected in the supervision, the worker is telling the supervisor what he had to endure in the interview.

The manifestations I have described so far are of straight identification. But there are other manifestations which I class differently. They are to do with identification, but not so directly, as it is a projection from the client which the worker accepts. There are many clients who cannot know about or hold big areas of their own feelings. It is the worker who comes away from the interview inappropriately worried, anxious and overburdened. The client feels better, but overnight the worker does not know that. The client has got rid of the bad feelings and the worker is left with them. The worker may either continue to carry them in the supervision, or he may, in his turn, attempt to get rid of them into the supervisor, who may then be the one left feeling weighed-down.

Searles is more explicit about what I have called the "for or against" in the countertransference, although he is tentative in suggesting what is the precise mechanism of the reflection. He says, "I feel most unsure and cannot, therefore, do more than tentatively suggest. As has been indicated, I believe that unconscious identification is one of the nuclear processes involved. It appears that the reflection process is initiated when the therapy touches upon an area of the patient's personality in which repressed or dissociated feelings are close to awareness, so that he simultaneously manifests anxiety and some defence against this anxiety. The therapist then, being exposed to the patient's anxiety, experiences a stirring up of his own anxiety with regard to the comparable area of his own personality. The therapist now, it seems, unconsciously copes with this anxiety in himself by either identifying with the defence-against-anxiety which the patient is utilising, or by resorting to a defence which is complementary to that which the patient is utilising."[2]

I differ from Searles in that I believe the reflection process can come into operation when the dissociated feelings are not close to awareness as well as when they are. But I think there is a big difference in the use that can be made of it. When the feelings are close to awareness in the client and the worker, the reflection can be put into words by the supervisor (when he becomes conscious of what is going on) and these words can be *heard*, discussed, and remembered by the worker. If he can be in touch with this feeling, and therefore have more understanding of what the client may be dissociating, his attitude is most likely to have changed when he next sees the client. By being less defended on this particular issue, he may send out quite different subliminal clues which the client, if his feelings are also near to the surface, will pick up. Then together, they will be able to find a shared and conscious understanding. The words will be very different from those used by the worker and supervisor, because they will be dictated more by the client's cultural background and educational level, and by his own particular facet of this feeling in relation to the problem which he has previously presented to the worker.

The first example which I give in the next chapter shows how the supervisor's reflection was of a feeling very near to consciousness. And very quickly she was able to change her stance and use her new understanding. Both this supervisor and the one in the second example show in their presentation the feeling they had introjected.

When, however, in this chain of client-worker-supervisor, the feeling at any point is too far from consciousness, the reflection may continue to defy understanding. If it is felt and perhaps understood, or partially understood, by only one person in the chain, the inability to make effective use of it will feel frustrating. The supervisor may be frustrated by the worker's not being able to pick up the link. Or the worker may be frustrated by the client's not being able to get near it. A persistently introjected feeling which cannot be passed back to its owner feels like a "foreign body". As Fordham says, when writing about countertransference, it can "deflect the worker from his aim at working at the level the client has reached. It is then easy to treat the client as if his defences do not exist."[3] And it can similarly deflect the supervisor from supervising at an appropriate level and from recognising his worker's defences. It is very easy in these circumstances to show too much "flair or intuition",[4] in an attempt to get rid of the introjection quickly.

The third example, *The Management of the Thumping*, in the next chapter, is an illustration of this type of difficulty. What I suspect was the most troublesome feeling of the clients was probably very repressed, although indirectly expressed in the material, but the group mainly acted out the defence, and, when it did get in touch with the feeling, was not able to make effective use of it, nor put the first glimmerings of understanding into words which could have been of help to the supervisor.

I am sure that many supervisors work with the reflection process without necessarily giving it this name and could quote numerous instances when they picked up the worker's over-identification or some feeling he had introjected from a client. What I want to stress is that I am not happy when these phenomena are taken to be just the weakness of the worker with a complementary denial of the strength of the psychopathology of many social work clients. If workers are led, even very subtly, to feel ashamed of their interaction and inability to withstand some of its grosser manifestations, their professional growth will be inhibited.

And if supervisors do not have to be above their own reactions, but can value them as "highly informative reflections of the relationship between client and worker,"[5] giving themselves a clearer realisation than any words could do of the pressure the client is exerting on the worker, they are more able to expose their supervision in detail and to continue to learn and to develop their teaching skills.

But, as I was saying in the last chapter, I do not think that the use of the countertransference needs to be restricted to diagnosis, nor that the actual acting-out of a countertransference reaction need be detrimental to the client. I was suggesting that it was sometimes positively helpful for the client if the worker went into the situation and was seen to get himself out of it. And I think the same is true in using the countertransference in the reflection process in supervision. A supervisor who is just an inactive mentor is giving an unfortunate model to his student. And it is the model, more often than the words, with which the student identifies. As I illustrated in the introduction, the reflection process works both ways and probably with even more intensity when the worker is a new student and desperately in need of a model with which to identify through his initial insecurity. This may be why many people say that it was their first supervisor who had such a profound effect upon them, much more so than any later ones.

The reflection process is obviously only a small part of supervision. But it is an important one which concerns the most difficult and disturbed cases. The more experienced the supervisor, the more aware he is of his own norm, then the more sensitively he can work with his own countertransference reaction and with the worker, and therefore with the case. In the Institute of Marital Studies we are only just starting to use this consciously in our teaching programmes. Our attempts are very fumbling and very crude. The examples in the next chapter show the limited start we have made in this direction.

CHAPTER FOUR

MANIFESTATIONS OF THE REFLECTION PROCESS

I am including four examples to illustrate some of the manifestations of the reflection process described in the last chapter. These examples, like the two given in the Introduction, are of seminar groups working on a supervision problem presented by one of the members. But they include much more detail of the case and of the discussion. The first example is given in the greatest detail and illustrates not only a very clear reflection process in operation, but also the way the group worked and the difficulties of sticking with the task when that task was studying "The Processes of Interaction". Although I have firmly edited the eighty original pages of the tape-recording transcript down to thirty, I have given a faithful account of the way in which the group tackled the material and the role I played in summarising the discussion and in emphasising certain points which needed to be understood by newer members before the group as a whole could take the discussion further forward.

I have wondered whether to edit the transcript even more tightly, leaving out much of the description of the case and of the discussion, abstracting only what I believed was a reflection of the case in the deadlock which the supervision had reached. But I decided against this for two reasons.

Firstly, I dislike books on casework which announce, for example, that after the fourth interview such and such happened, apparently miraculously. I am left unconvinced, not knowing how or why it had, and not at all sure that any fundamental piece of work could be so easy. As I emphasised in the introductory and third chapters, our attempts at working in this way are still very crude. I do not want to leave the impression that detailed work with unconscious processes can ever be easy or slick. So I have decided to leave in the text the struggle to understand—the failures and the partial failures of understanding—alongside the glimpses of recognition of something important. And example III is one of failure when the reflection proved a "foreign body" (page 47) and we were unable to make effective use of it in the group. In all the examples I have left enough of the detail of the case and of the supervision, so that the reader can make up his own mind about the validity of the thesis. It is impossible to illustrate the reflection process without giving considerable detail of what it is that is reflected, and it cannot be separated from the larger task of considering other interactive processes within the work.

This relates to my second reason. As I said in the third chapter, the use of the reflection process is obviously only a small part of supervision. And I do not want to take the reflection process out of its wider context. Certainly in seminars for supervisors we use it in trying to understand why an otherwise competent supervisor feels stuck in supervising a particular case. But this occurrence is often most acute when the case symbolises, or highlights, what are more general difficulties of many students and young workers, and of many supervisors, either in the process of supervision, or in the working structure. All the examples indirectly illustrate general and perennial problems. Examples I and III illustrate the supervisor's problem of the autonomy of the worker—how much can the supervisor interfere? Example I also illustrates the difficulty of supervising one's co-worker. Example II highlights the problem of many students of whether they should, or can dare to, get involved. Example IV illustrates the extreme difficulty when the reflection of a case compounds the feelings about a difficulty in the working structure. I do not think that these types of problem can be solved in general terms, but only in relation to particular pieces of work. In leaving the discussion of these problems in the text, I am illustrating my view that it is more meaningful to learn from the particular to the general, rather than the other way round; and I am attempting not to get the reflection process (despite the necessary emphasis in writing to the title of this monograph) out of its proper context.

Examples II, III and IV are shorter, and increasingly I have paraphrased the discussion, giving only enough of the direct speech to give the reader the atmosphere and tone. I hope the longer text of the first example is explanatory of later, shortened statements about the group's behaviour.

Each example is preceded by a short introduction and followed by my comment on certain points which illustrate the main thesis and basic assumptions outlined in previous chapters. I have decided not to place the comment here and there in the text, except for some short interspersions to draw attention to some particularly important statement or juxtaposition, as I know many people find this irritating, and prefer to do their own thinking about the material while they read. The comment at the end, however, refers back to numbered paragraphs and to page numbers in Chapters II and III, so that readers can immediately turn back to the relevant part of the text.

After the comment on each example, I give a postscript about the subsequent work with the case. Then there is a short summary for readers who are interested only in the thesis and not in the detailed working out of its application by a typical group of supervisors of varying ability and experience. Some readers may prefer to give themselves a strong signpost through the text of the detailed work by reading the summary first.

In each example, the supervisor and the worker are of well above average ability. For people of less professional competence and confidence, this detailed exposure of their work would be too difficult. With the two London based groups, I knew something of the supervisors' standard of work from at least one year's experience of working with them on their own cases in thirty seminars. With the Devon supervisors, I had known their work over a much longer period, which made it easier to pick up when they were acting out of character.

Example I

EITHER-OR

This example shows a very clear reflection by a student and a supervisor of the behaviour of two clients with whom they worked, the student with the husband, the supervisor with the wife. The supervisor had got stuck on an argument which had the same quality of "either/or" —you do, or you don't—so typical of the arguments between the two clients. The countertransference of the two workers was "for" their own client and "against" the other client, which is usual.

The feelings the supervisor defended against were very near to consciousness, and very quickly she was able to change her stance. But before the group was able to look in detail at what was being reflected, they had to work on the case and explore the homosexual elements in the interaction between the couple and their workers.

This example highlights two problems: firstly, the difficulty of supervising one's co-worker; and secondly, the amount of autonomy a student can be allowed.

Readers who want a series of signposts through the discussion are advised to turn to the summary on page 74.

THE CASE OF JACK AND LORNA HILL

Presenting:	Probation Officer:	Mrs Katherine Anderson
Worker:	Student:	Mr George Clark; two-year graduate course
Family:	Husband:	Mr Jack Hill, aged 26, lorry driver by trade; one year sentence being served in open prison
	Wife:	Mrs Lorna Hill, aged 29, housewife; three years probation for larceny
	Children:	Terence Brown, aged 11, Lorna's child of previous marriage
		Matthew Hill, aged 4 ⎱ children of the
		Diana Hill, aged 1 ⎰ marriage

Mrs Anderson is an experienced, middle-aged probation officer, who is not easily fooled. She does not waste words and speaks slowly and very much to the point with a slightly caustic and self-depreciating humour. Often her eyes gleam meaningfully as she illustrates her point with an expressive grimace and accompanying movement of her hand.

First she described to the seminar group the case with which she had worked for two years. She had brought Mr Clark into the work three months previously when he started his final placement of the course with an expressive grimace and accompanying movement of her hand. prison, and she had continued to work with Lorna.

"Well, first I'll start with Lorna. She is twenty-nine and she's got 3
three children. She's married to Jack, who is twenty-seven. Lorna's
appearance is important. She is very, very small. When she's fat,
she weighs six and a half stone.

"When she is what?" 4

"When she is fat. When she is fat, she weighs six and a half stone, 5
but generally she weighs about four or five pounds under six stone.
And, because she is so tiny, she can look intensely girlish and feminine,
but very much like a little girl. One of her complaints is that her bust
is only thirty-one inches, and this is a source of great concern to her.

"When things go wrong, she dons men's clothes. The moment she 6
comes in the door wearing men's clothes, then I know we've got problems. But when she comes in looking very pretty in her mini-skirt, then
I know things aren't too bad.

"This is her second marriage. She was first married when she was 7
eighteen, and her husband lived with her until two days before Terence
was born. He walked out and never came back. He pays her regularly
£2 a week for Terence and has never defaulted. Five years later she
married Jack, and she has two children by him, Matthew, four years
old, and Diana, one year old. Matthew and Diana were born when
Jack was in prison.

"In between the two marriages Lorna coped marvellously. She got 8
herself a job, she found somebody to look after Terence and she found
herself a room in the house owned by Jack's mother. So she saw a
lot of Jack in a very legitimate way. She didn't pick him up and their
friendship grew. And while it was growing, Jack's mother said, 'Lorna
isn't good enough for my Jack.' And Lorna took up this challenge and
eventually married Jack and, as she says, 'to spite' her mother-in-law.
But I also think she married him for more cogent reasons. He is marvellous with Terence, accepting him totally and getting more pleasure
out of him at that age than he does out of his own children.

"Jack is a great lump of slow-thinking, slow-moving, overgrown boy. 9
A great lump of a boy. And if things don't go right with him, then,
face it, he gives up and he slobbers and Mum comforts him. So every
time anything goes wrong, he flies to his mother and this makes Lorna
extremely angry.

"Jack does not work. The only thing he will do is to drive the biggest 10
lorries. He is a very good driver. But he won't drive a van. He will
drive a sixty-foot articulated lorry or nothing. But he hasn't got a heavy
goods vehicle licence."

"Why can't he get a licence if he's a good driver?" 11

"Well, about two years ago, he got two endorsements on his licence 12
for not having sufficient rubber on the tyres. He was driving for a firm,
and although his licence was endorsed, any normal firm would know

that it wasn't his responsibility to that extent. But, because he's got two endorsements, he won't drive until the three years are up and his licence is free of them. His pride won't allow him to show his licence to anybody because of the two endorsements. And he cannot get his heavy goods vehicle licence because he wasn't driving for a living during the relevant qualification period. So because of his behaviour towards his two endorsements, he's cut himself off from work and from getting the licence he wanted.

"Terence identifies very strongly with Jack. But Matthew is very   13
like Jack and Jack's mother delights in him. Lorna is terrified lest Matthew gets the 'Jack-treatment' from her mother-in-law, turning him into a non-working criminal.

"Lorna's offence was burglary, committed with her cousin. She was   14
the look-out and took the goods handed to her. Jack planned it with them, but did not participate because he was on a suspended sentence. She then confronted him with his lack of virility. And she emphasises his inferior position by making it clear that, while she will permit intercourse, she does not enjoy it. Jack demonstrates his frustration by going on occasional drinking bouts, refusing to allow her to get a job and by returning to his mother. He does, however, remain faithful to her. At the time her probation order was made, she was in her most masculine role, wearing masculine clothes.

"Jack has got four previous convictions. The circumstances of his   15
third offence were that he and Lorna quarrelled. He was trying to make it up with her and she would have nothing to do with him. While they were out she saw a little Skye terrier with a bow on the top of its head and said that was what she wanted. And Jack went back to his mother and they could not make it up. About a month later he came back with a Skye terrier with a bow on its head and complete with harness. She immediately returned the dog. And then he went to prison again after a charge of receiving.

"Lorna and Jack have a deep-seated matrimonial problem. Lorna has   16
a great fear of being pregnant. She has very difficult births, probably because she is so very tiny. Whenever Jack does a 'job', his immediate reaction is to get Lorna pregnant. So the pattern has been that he does a burglary and within a month Lorna's pregnant. He expects to be caught, wants to keep her firmly anchored, and, sure enough, by the time he gets to Quarter Sessions or to Crown Court, Lorna's four or five months' pregnant. He goes in quite joyfully and has a rest from it all. He comes out when the baby's there. This he acknowledges is his plan.

"Last time he did this, he did the 'job' in August. In September   17
Lorna came to me and said, 'I'm sure I'm pregnant.' And I said, 'What makes you so sure?' And she said, 'Jack's got a summons, Jack's

got to go to Court.' And she was pregnant. Jack got bail and during that time she got herself a back-street abortion which was very dangerous. But she was delighted because, at last, she'd foiled Jack and she wasn't going to have a baby while he was inside. And she went to Quarter Sessions and appeared before the Recorder and he thought she was going to make a plea on Jack's behalf. She went up there and she said, 'What you want to do with this man is not to send him to prison, because he likes that. Make him stay outside and support me and the kids.' The Recorder was horrified and sent Jack down, which reinforced Lorna's opinion that all men were the biggest fools she could see.

"So Jack went to prison and Lorna decided that she was having 18 nothing to do with him. She was going to sort herself out. The day before he went to Quarter Sessions he stole the rent money which she is meticulous about paying. He went on the booze with it. I tried to get her to see why he did this, but she was very cross with me and then I joined the category of stupid males.

"She has now got the whole of her affairs in apple-pie order. She's 19 got the rent up to date. She's been to Social Security. She's got clothes for the kids. She's terribly proud of the fact that she's managing marvellously without 'that one up there'." (The open prison is on a hill above the town where Lorna lives.)

"He said he would like to go to open prison. He was no escape risk 20 and there were plenty of places. He is doing his 'bird' in the most comfortable surroundings. His mother goes every time he sends a visiting order. She puts a £1 note in a piece of silver paper, puts it in her mouth, kisses Jack goodbye, transfers the note over to his mouth and he can get a bit more extra baccy. And he writes the most loving and enticing letters to Lorna, asking her to go and visit."

Mrs Anderson took breath and at last introduced the student into 21 this account. "He is being supervised by my student who is terribly fearful that this marriage is going to break up. My student is newly married and his wife is pregnant. He has a terrible fear that Lorna is going to leave Jack and he is very angry with me because I won't, in fact, instruct Lorna to go up to the prison. I have given the student permission to talk to Lorna, to discuss with her whether she would join in a joint interview which he is very keen on having, but not with me; he doesn't want me there. He feels that I would obviously topple it over. He wants to see just the two of them in prison. I have warned him of the pitfalls, but I have said that if this is really what he wants to do, and provided Lorna agrees, he can go ahead with it and arrange it. And he's got Lorna's permission to arrange it with the Governor. But she is very angry with the student because she sees these two men being very close together and manipulating her. She agreed, but she says, 'If I go up there, I'm going to spill the dirt.' And that means that she's going to diminish Jack in front of the student. And this has left the student very worried. He doesn't know what he is going to hear from Lorna. So that is where we are."

Mrs Anderson paused, but before the group could intervene, she 22 emphasised again that she did not think that Lorna had any intention of leaving Jack. "She's just continuing the punishment and she's making up for what the Court did not give him. She doesn't answer his letters, but she does go up there on a visiting order. But she never tells him whether she is going or not.

"And so we're, you know, all muddled up with Jack's needs and 23 Lorna's needs and the need of my student to be reassured . . . and you don't punish your wife when you give her a baby . . . and . . . ." Mrs Anderson's voice slowed down and then petered out, expressing the muddle between herself and the student. "You can't sort of . . . you can't sort of use babies in this fashion. And the student . . . he's unwilling to be convinced that Jack does in fact do this."

The group could not take up the problem of the student and Mrs 24 Anderson immediately. First they needed to clarify parts of the material. And they started where Mrs Anderson left off—on the student's lack of conviction on the subject of the babies—of Lorna's conceiving Matthew and Diana when Jack had done a 'job'. Some of the members joined the student in disbelief that this could happen and they queried whether Lorna had conceived before or after the offence.

"I'm not clear why she gets pregnant just at the time that she does." 25

"Do women just get pregnant, just like that, or do they want to get 26 pregnant when they do?"

"It happens when he gets himself away?" 27

"Or does he get himself away when it happens?" 28

"He does it beforehand," said Mrs Anderson, "so that at the time of 29 the offence he has no expectation of being a successful criminal." (The confusion, probably of the clients, and of the group, here seems to get into Mrs Anderson. It is not clear what the "it" he does beforehand is. In her initial presentation she was perfectly clear that the baby was conceived after the offence.)

Assuming the "it" to be the intercourse which conceived the baby, 30 another member said, "So he gets himself away for the birth. What do you read into this—a cowardly approach to a crisis?"

"No, more that Lorna is much more intelligent than he is, much more 31 deceptive and much more able to talk. And he sees Lorna as a terrible threat to his ability to assert himself, to his masculinity. She is a terrible threat. She won't permit him intercourse if she can help it. She avoids intercourse with him." (Has Mrs Anderson picked up, but been unable to find words beyond that of "threat", to describe his envy, alongside his assertion of his masculinity, that it is the women, not the men, who bear the children?) She continued about the difficulty over contraception. When Lorna got her supply of pills, Jack crushed them up. That was his favourite way of using the pill. Lorna wanted to be sterilised, but Jack would not agree to this. He controlled her by getting her pregnant and the intercourse after the offence had felt like "rape" to Lorna.

"But these two are just like overgrown children. But she's not so 32 overgrown. She's a little girl and she's happiest when she and Jack are romping around with their own children and Terence, and this is what she says is the happiest part of her life and that's when she really likes Jack.

"She said that every Saturday night—and she was ashamed to tell 33 me this—that every Saturday night Jack baths the three kids and then he baths her, and he insists on doing this every single Saturday night. And he wraps her up in a blanket and they go downstairs in front of the fire and he makes her a hot drink. And then they go to bed. 'But then,' she says, 'he spoils it all, because he then wants to make love.' And she just wants to cuddle up to him and be a little girl."

"Does Jack treat her as a daughter or a wife?" 34

"A sister, I think. A younger sister. Yes, a very much younger sister. 35 Slightly incestuous."

This theme of Jack getting Lorna pregnant, of controlling her and 36 getting himself away was returned to several times and eventually Lorna's part in this was noted. It had happened in her first marriage as well. Then she was without her husband—he deserted two days previously—when she gave birth to Terence. Then we learnt that generally "she puts other women as a barrier. I've never seen a man in her house and I've called at the oddest times. But mainly the house is full of women. She fills the house with women who get between her and Jack and between her and me. I've taken this up with her and she can see this is what she is doing. She's always saying to Jack, 'Why don't you go off and get another woman who likes it?' But he's always faithful to her. Jack is convinced that Lorna is not going to have him back. She says she does not want him back, but instinct tells me that they'll be back."

One of the group members then asked if there was any violence or 37 threat of violence between the two of them.

"Yes, she's often, she's often had to leave the house screaming when 38 he's beaten her up. But she enjoys this bit of being beaten, because this really shows Jack up, that he isn't the great, slow-moving, love-able slob that everyone thinks he is. He's the violent, 'horrible man who beats me up, a little woman'. And she makes sure that all the neighbours know, that the rent collector knows, that the welfare knows, and everybody knows."

The question of punishment and control was left for the time being   39
and the group asked for some more history. "Jack's father is a real,
what I call a real, old-fashioned farm-labourer. Yes, he's still alive,
but very much under his wife's thumb, and one of Jack's cries to
Lorna is, 'You're never going to get me like my Dad is.' Lorna's
family is very respectable. Her father is dead. She has ideas about her
father that he was the most marvellous father, he kept them all in order,
he was a good disciplinarian, he took them out on Sundays, he did
odd jobs about the house and he had a steady job until the day he died.
'Yes, and he died young, didn't he?' says Jack. She had two older
sisters and her family really wanted a boy, and, one gathers, she acted
the part of a tomboy."

"And she was still doing the same when she met Jack."   40
"Yes, and she still does it now."   41
A member of the group again tried to get back to the subject of   42
punishment. "I'm not clear whether she is trying to punish Jack or
whether Jack is trying to punish her. I mean, it depends on which
way you look at it. I mean is she acting out something for herself
through Jack which allows . . . which pushes him to commit these
offences? Or is it Jack who has a need to punish her?"

"Punish her or control her?"   43
"Well, I would have thought that there would . . . there must . . . be   44
such a lot of anger in Jack against women. Really, I mean, this sloppy
old mum. I wonder how he really feels about her."

"He may not be letting Lorna do to him what his mother did to his   45
father, but he's certainly letting his mother do to him what she did to
his father."

"But mum buys off his anger."   46
"Very difficult to be angry with a mother who puts a £1 note literally   47
into your mouth."

"Yes, and a kiss with it."   48
"It must be a peculiar kind of kiss."   49
"Last week my student told me that Jack had sent a £1 to Lorna for   50
her to buy something—one of his mother's £ notes. And Lorna sent it
back and pointed out that as he'd got it illegally and it didn't come
through on a prison envelope, she didn't think she ought to keep it,
which was her way of making sure that he got into trouble for that one."

Again the group retreated, ignoring the student and his part in the   51
work—retreated to Lorna's size and to her clothing, apparently mes-
merized by her weighing "six and a half stone when she's fat". "Yes,
she is, you know, she looks like . . . to see her at a distance . . . you
know how a child walks with rather stiff arms, particularly when
they're playing that game of not stepping on the cracks in the pave-
ment. You know how kids won't walk. She walks humpity like that.

And that's her normal walk. Very girlish, and she tried to get herself a miscarriage once by falling off a swing at a playground."

"When you say she's in trouble, as it were, she wears men's clothing, 52 really men's clothing or just jeans?"

"No, really men's clothing. Masculine. She'll wear a shirt with long 53 sleeves, which is totally unlike her normal, feminine side. And she gives the impression of being a young man."

"Presumably they can't be Jack's clothes?" 54

"No. She has this selection of clothing. I never knew where she 55 got them from, but I have taken it up and now she can come in and make a joke about it. 'Oh, God,' she'll say, 'I ought to have put my dress on and then you wouldn't have thought I was doing so badly, would you?' But she sees this dress business as important. But now she's missing Jack and she is having fantasies that she could, you know, find another man.

"She took the children to a Christmas party arranged by the local 56 council. And there was a man there who was ferrying these children from home. And he said to Lorna, 'Can I take you home?' And she said to me that she'd seen him at the party so she thought he was all right. So he took her home and she made coffee for him. And since then he's been visiting her and she thought he was Mr Salter from the social service department. She was delighted. She said, 'He's old, he's older than you,' which I thought was charming. 'Older than you, you know, but he treats me like a little girl.' It was quite astonishing, you see, because there we were both falling into this same trap. It was only when I realised that he didn't leave till half past eleven did it begin to dawn. Then he said he wasn't Mr Salter; he was a member of the Rotary who was helping at the party. She wished he'd go away, but she kept saying to me, 'Well, you know, it's lonely in the evenings.' "

"Does she push you into treating her like a little girl?" 57

"No. I don't treat her like a little girl. I'm very aware of this." 58

"*What about the student?*" (At last, at last.) 59

"The student—she fell head over heels in love with this bearded 60 student, and came careering round to me and thanked me for sending him. The whole neighbourhood was agog. But the moment she saw how related he was to Jack, she rapidly went off him. So she's content to have me."

"You say that the student is desperate that the marriage is going to 61 break. Why is he in such a state? What's he picked up from Jack?"

"Jack is communicating this and he is a great believer in having 62 things done for him. He wants something done about his marriage. And looking at it and being away from it isn't helping Jack, so he thinks. (In these and the following sentences Jack and the student become fused and it is not always clear of which one Mrs Anderson is speaking.) He thinks the only way his marriage can be healed is if somebody does something. And if Jack can't get out to go and see Lorna, well, then we've got to have Lorna going up to the prison and make her face Jack. He really is wanting to use the student to say, 'Now Lorna, you go back, because Jack has promised to change.' ''

"And is this particular to this case—that he can't resist having to   63
do his client's bidding, doing the reconciling?"

"He still has difficulty in using himself in the situation. He feels   64
he hasn't had any experience, which is true. He's very reserved and will, I feel, fall into a trap of doing, not being. He is very insecure at the moment and this is making him very anxious to prove that he can mend this marriage. He has no confidence that they'll go back together again."

"It sounds to me in many ways as if you're both very much on the   65
side of your clients, seeing the other one as the nigger in the woodpile. He's seeing Lorna as playing things up and you're seeing Jack as being the louse."

"Yes, I know this. I made this clear to him that I was identifying   66
with Lorna, but felt that she needed Jack. He didn't think it was enough to feel, to have these feelings about it. His reaction was, 'Well, what are you going to do about it?' And I said I was going to do nothing about it, which then makes him feel very angry with me. Because I'm sort of adopting Lorna's attitude. I was going to sit back and look at this, use this bit of separation to look at it."

There was then a big flight from the work of Mrs Anderson and   67
the student, one member expressing concern that he could not see Jack and Lorna's "relationship with the outside world", that Jack could not pursue his trade and get a heavy goods vehicle licence, that the doctor would not allow her a sterilisation, that "these blocks from society are keeping them fixed in their position. They don't seem to have any power to sort of alter their own lives at all, and immediately retreat into having more babies and not working."

Up to this point I had participated very little in the discussion. But   68
now I would not allow this flight. We did know that two endorsements did not mean that a person could not drive; rather it was Jack's feelings about the endorsements, or, perhaps, even his fear of leaving home and being out of the house when Lorna was not safely pregnant, which prevented him, the endorsements providing a rationalisation. And we had heard that it was Jack, not the doctor, who would not let Lorna be sterilised. But I did think that the idea of the "fix" was important. I went back over some of the previous discussion on the unconscious homosexuality in this case, Jack's difficult relationship with his mother, the anger which he could not express directly to her about keeping him a

baby and so indulging him, and of Lorna's having to be the boy and yet keeping herself surrounded by women. Both of them were trying to grow up and become more heterosexual, but when it got difficult both of them retreated into a homosexual position, she into her men's clothes and her organising, and he into a position of being looked after, and both of them being very punishing to the other. The group had queried whether she was acting-out something for herself through Jack which pushed him out to commit these offences. Was she punishing Jack, or was he punishing her, they had asked. I queried whether it had to be a question of "either/or". "Does it have to be mutually exclusive? Perhaps with this couple, both of them punish and undermine the other. But, if one person has got to be punished, there must be something in the other that will continue over a period of time to go along with this and let themselves be punished. He is punishing her and also punishing himself, as he punished himself on the driving. And she is very punishing to him in prison." I went back over the interactive theme of "the offences and the babies—to do with them both; he may have to try and keep her broody[1] and then get out of the way, but there is also something about Lorna that it has happened with two husbands— that she didn't have the husband and father around when she had the babies.

"It happened with another man, too," I emphasized. I knew that   69
most of the group understood this, but I emphasized it for the new members who had joined the workshop that year.

I went back to the idea of a "fix". I thought Mrs Anderson's work   70
with Lorna had helped to undo a bit of this fix. After the last offence Lorna had not gone along with being left pregnant. Her methods may have been dangerous, but within her culture, all that may have been available to her, and she had changed the previous pattern. But the present fix seemed to be about punishment. (Mrs Anderson had finished her initial presentation on the theme of punishment. "She's just continuing the punishment and she's making up for what the Court did not give him." It was then she had started to stumble and had lost her clarity.) I wondered if this had got into the supervision and into the presentation and discussion. Was the present fix about punishing the one who was pushed out? Jack was safely away in prison and the student had hardly been mentioned. And where could we get into the fix to unstick it a bit? "Where can Katherine and the student put in a bit of work which will unglue this a bit?"

"But even if the fix is there in their relationship, I mean aren't   71
there other ways of dealing with it?" asked one new member despairingly. "I mean why can't a man in an open prison get his driving training while he's there?"

The discussion moved to the open prison. "The best thing you can   72 hope for on a parole licence is to go off on an H.G.V. training course of one week, if you are lucky."

But another member brought the discussion back to the couple.   73

"What you were getting at just now, Jan, that we've been talking   74
about this couple fighting each other, but, in fact, they're working very hard at creating a co-operative set-up."

"Yes, they're incredibly co-operative, keeping it in a fix," added   75
another.

"Even the old judge got into the fix when he sent him down."   76

"Jack was delighted to go down," said Mrs Anderson.   77

"But Lorna got herself an abortion. So now here's Jack, stewing   78
away up on the hillside, looking down over the town, wondering what his wife is up to. She's no longer safe with a baby. And somehow he's building all this into the student."

"He's lost control over her. Instead of lumbering her seven or eight   79
months' pregnant and being unattractive, she's entertaining a mysterious social worker. He must be in a bait."

"But," said Mrs Anderson, "when he gets into a bait he smashes   80
things up or he commits an offence."

"But certainly this is getting into the student with tremendous . . ."   81

"And Jack's turned him into his Mum to put it right."   82

"What are the achievable goals in this interview? What sort of way   83
would you like to see it going?"

"I can't see much future for this interview," Mrs Anderson replied.   84

"But why have you allowed yourself to get pushed out and not go   85
there with Lorna?"

"I didn't want to go there. I said from the beginning, 'A bit of me   86
doesn't agree with dragging Lorna up the hill.' "

"But you're making sure that the student will get finished off by   87
Lorna. Has he got experience to do this interview on his own?"

"I do think it will be a destructive interview," Mrs Anderson said,   88
"but, before the arrangements were made, I went through the possible consequences with him."

"I don't see why it need be a destructive interview," I intervened.   89
"There has been one big shift in the fix which means that prison is not such a cushy number for Jack. Things aren't going according to plan, but . . ."

"But I think it will be destructive," said a member, "because my   90
guess is that Jack will take out his anger with his mother and the student will take out his anger with you on Lorna, because it sounds as if it is getting a bit sort of . . . yukky . . . between the two of you, at least where this case is concerned."

"No, not specially," Mrs Anderson said. She described how the   91
student had, after seeing Jack, wanted to work with Lorna as well.

They had discussed this at some length, but Mrs Anderson had felt it would be wrong for her to hand over Lorna when, after a long period, she had started to build up a good working relationship with her. "She took probation because it was a soft option, but she didn't really want it. She saw it as a three-year slog." Mrs Anderson had offered to take back Jack, but Mr Clark's immediate reaction had been, " 'I don't want to give up Jack, because I think I can influence Lorna.' I thought, 'This is highly dangerous.' " (Again note that it is not clear whether Mrs Anderson is talking about Jack or the student.) At this point I supported Mrs Anderson in holding on to her client, but I thought it was very real and more heterosexual that Jack was feeling jealous and fearful of what Lorna was doing outside while he was in prison. I wondered what the main issue of the interview would be.

But the discussion continued on the anxiety rather than the content— 92 the student's anxiety and the group's anxiety about this interview. They thought any important issue to the couple would be avoided because Lorna might be seen to punish Jack in the eyes of the student, and it would not get any further than that. Mrs Anderson said that she was worried about the effect on Jack. He was worried about his relationship with Lorna. If he could stick to that point, she did not see that this interview need be destructive. "Only to the student," she said, "if it gets too much for him."

It was now time to end the seminar, but it was decided that as we had 93 now just got to the crunch and to the point of Mrs Anderson's present anxiety about the student's work, that we would continue into another session. This we had had to do on several occasions when the discussion needed to cover the actual case, the work of the student and the supervision.

We resumed after coffee and I opened the session, summarising where 94 the previous discussion had got to—the shift in the situation. This prison sentence was different from previous ones, because Lorna was not safe with a baby; the subsequent anxiety was more noticeable in Jack, but probably, I thought, belonged to Lorna as well. Change was bound to produce anxiety. In her determination to hang on to change on Lorna's behalf, allowing her freedom of choice, Mrs Anderson was not going to be made "to drag her up the hill". It sounded as if it felt to her as if she was being made to do something. (Here, I think, I fused Mrs Anderson and Lorna, as it is Lorna who is being pressed to go, and Mrs Anderson who has refused to do the dragging.) I suggested that Lorna was probably very split in her feelings, wanting to go and enjoying being pressed, and at the same time not wanting to go and wanting to stick to her original intention. Perhaps, as she had decided to go, Mrs Anderson carried the latter feeling for her—the bit that did not want to go. But this interview might, and could, be productive if it could focus on the present anxiety arising from the present changed position. Was the anxiety the group was feeling on behalf of the student—that he was going to feel dreadful if nothing came of it—something to do with the anxiety in the case at this particular point in time? Could the change be maintained and not be too destructive?

A member expressed two worries; firstly, whether the student could 95 cope with this interview on his own; and secondly, that Jack would be supported by his worker, and Lorna would not be, and so might be that much more defensive and therefore give "Jack a more difficult run on this."

There was discussion on whether the difficulties could be anticipated 96 —could the student "be given some armour, some forewarning"—and on whether the prison setting would make this interview feel safer for the two clients than if they were in their own home.

"But I'm a bit confused," said one member, "because we've got to 97 thinking it's Katherine who says she's not going, but didn't you say at the beginning that the student didn't want you there?"

"He didn't. He wasn't thinking originally of it being a foursome. 98 And I had said that if both parties had thought it a good idea, if Lorna had said she wanted to talk to Jack, but she wasn't seeing it as useful . . ."

"Why's she going?"   99

"To prove, I think, to prove that she can survive this. Which is why 100 you're probably right and she's likely to be defensive, but attacking at the same time from her defensive position. She's so angry that he's escaping his responsibilities. She really wants to be a protected, feminine, little person. And then she had to abandon this role and look after the children and take on responsibility for everything. And she says, 'He wants to be made to be outside. He wants to be made to work.' She says, 'He's got to prove that he's a worthy man before I have him back.' She says she's going to pull the rosy tinted spectacles off the student's eyes."

I took the discussion back to the speaker who had reminded us 101 that the student did not want Mrs Anderson at this interview. For a time we had heard only her disapproval of the idea. But the split in the case was in the two workers, Katherine's not wanting to be at this interview and the student's not wanting her there. I suggested, "You are in an extremely difficult position in this. With two workers on the case the fight is likely to get into the two of you. It isn't odd that your student is so identifying with Jack and is fighting you, or that it gets into you when your client is saying, 'While he's in prison, I'm leading my own efficient life on my own.' But the added complication is that you supervise your co-worker and you also have a responsibility for him and his learning. One way of letting him learn is through his own mistakes. And this is fair enough if he can hold the situation well enough to see where he's made a mistake and see it through and get out the other side, in the process having learnt that it doesn't help Jack to do his work for him. But, on the other hand, it doesn't help him to learn if he comes a cropper on this threesome interview." I again emphasized the homosexual elements in the case and what a lot Lorna had been getting from Katherine; initially she had probably got more from a woman social worker than Jack had. I thought it good that Jack had now got a man worker. One common unconscious homosexual fantasy was that it needed two men to be able to cope with one dangerous woman. This had probably got into the student from Jack, which was his part of wanting to exclude Katherine. But she was going along with this and somehow couldn't resolve her disagreement with the student.

"Perhaps it's fanciful," said another member, "but I keep drawing 102 the analogy between Jack sending out the £1 and Lorna sending it back and getting him into trouble, and you're sending Lorna up there alone to get the student into trouble. Perhaps it's fanciful, but I keep on seeing this." (i.e. the reflection.)

"In some ways the student is innocent in the situation," said Mrs 103 Anderson, "but I think his innocence is his strength, why Lorna has responded and is going there. It might be quite important that he is going to throw them together. He has very genuine feelings for Jack, but at an earlier date, a little over confidently, he reassured Jack that everything would be fine. This is the hook he's now finding himself on. And his anxiety about leaving, of course. He wants this to be all tidied up before he goes, you know. And he has feelings about me not loving Jack and only loving Lorna."

"And you think he doesn't really have to worry about that?" 104

"No, but it's real for him." 105

"Everybody seems to think this interview is going to be disastrous. 106 But what's going to happen? What's the worst that can happen?"

"An abject sense of failure." 107

"For whom?" 108

"What would it do to you, Katherine, if the student asks Lorna up 109 to the camp and they have a very significant interview and you are left, away, not part of it?"

"It would reassure me, honestly—not necessarily relating to my 110 work with Lorna, but a reassurance for me in my work with the student —but they're so intermixed."

"I wanted to ask you, how fearful is the student of the aggression 111 between these two? And is he aggressive with you? Is he afraid of this?"

"No, there is a total lack of aggression. He gets depressed, but there 112 is no aggression that one picks up. No verbal aggression."

5

"But that staggers me," said the student's university tutor. "Verbally 113 he can be as aggressive as any we've got." And later she said, "Are we really talking about the same person?" In the presentation of this case he came across very differently from the person she knew and whom she had taught.

Mrs Anderson explained that her so easily opting out of this interview 114 was something to do with her feeling of not wanting to over-supervise, "never letting him on the loose".

"Maybe," said someone, "but he's trying to get into the work with 115 the marriage."

"Yes, he wants to take the two of them and sort it out between them. 116 And my feelings are that if a person reaches a stage when they feel they can only complete their work by taking a certain course, by all means prepare them for it, but I think they need the personal freedom to take this course."

"Yes, I agree with you," I said, "but this is very much easier to put 117 into practice when the student is working singly. But on this case you are co-workers as well as student and supervisor. And it reminds me of the way we usually work with two workers and the disagreements that we have. It reminds me very much of a case I have at the moment with a less experienced worker. He is always wanting a double inter-view—a foursome. And we have been arguing about this because I said, 'No, not at the moment. At the moment I have got to work with my client in singles and it's at a very tricky stage and I'm not having it ruined by a foursome too early.' And I've been hanging on to this, but it's easier for me to argue with him, because I don't supervise him. But when the dynamics of the case get into the working pair, you can't ignore it. But it needs to be solved with the working pair before it has a chance of getting solved in the marriage. I think I am afraid that with the student doing this interview on his own, you both act out with the couple the split between you and your student—your fight, your disagreement. It is unlikely that the student will be able to do any inter-pretative work, so an awful lot depends on the model presented to them. Does that make sense?" I asked tentatively, fearful that I had been over-teaching.

But I went on, however, anticipating the interview. It could be a non- 118 event; or it could be very helpful if there was a bit more understanding of what went on between them and what they were up to; or it could be destructive. "Lorna might fling the other non-existent men at Jack— the being lonely in the evenings. But the important bit that you have, Katherine, is that you know, and she knows that you know, that, in fact, when it comes to the point it is the women who are more im-portant."

I continued speaking, using some of my own experience and a case 119 which my colleague and I had presented at the previous workshop in which there was a strong, punishing, sadistic element in one of the clients, and my concern about joint interviews with this type of couple. I said I was worried about the interview with Jack and Lorna if it was one-sided, and one client was less supported and therefore more defensive and more attacking. "I suppose," I said, "I am backing your skill more than the student's to deal with this sort of thing."

Mrs Anderson expressed concern that Lorna was much more articu- 120 late than Jack and that this would be reflected in her and the student. "Inarticulate old Jack—new student, and articulate Lorna and old me."

Again there was surprise expressed by the university tutor that the 121 student could not hold his own in his own way. There was a short attempt to get a more all round picture of the student not so coloured by his reflection of Jack.

The discussion moved back to the confusion when co-worker and 122 supervisor were one person. "It's interesting that you can't say 'no' to your student in the way Janet can say 'no' to her co-worker, because your student is dependent on you."

In the final seminar of this workshop, when we were pulling some 123 things together that had arisen on several of the students' supervised cases, this subject came up again, and Mrs Anderson stressed the importance of the autonomy of the student in the probation service. "I could not with any student say, 'Now, look here, I say, No.' " And, going back to this case and this student, she gave an interesting piece of interaction from one of the supervisory sessions, depicting her reaction to the student's reflection of Jack. "I said, 'Look'— in fact these were my words—'You really are putting me in a position now of being your probation officer. My duty as a probation officer is to make you aware as best I can of the consequences of your action. Really you are putting me in that position. Now if you have thought about the consequences of this interview, well then, go ahead and do it, but remember a), b), c), etc.' "

This, I thought, was the wrong use of autonomy. "This is all right," 124 I said, "if neither Jack nor Lorna are married and Jack is just your student's client. But you have got a married couple here and if we are using our understanding of marital interaction and it is the inter-action that is important, then you've got to stop talking about the autonomy of one client. Is it appropriate to talk about the autonomy of the student in relation to one client when you've opted to work the marital case with two workers?" I went back to the clients who seemed very "either/or". Jack could drive with a clear licence, or not at all with an endorsement. It couldn't be known that there was something in between; you could drive with one or two endorsements. I wondered if this either/or quality got into the supervision. It had got into this discussion group, in which the members were used to working with the interaction. Even a most experienced member had questioned the either/or of who was punishing whom, as if we had had a decision to make. It seemed to me that Mrs Anderson felt that either the student had complete autonomy, or that he had to be forbidden. Letting a student learn through some of his own mistakes did not mean that the supervisor had to let him come a complete cropper. *This bit of punishing on her part, which had got into her from this case, and which had got confused with the either/or element, and then with her feelings about the autonomy of the probation officer, gave us an even stronger indication of the strength of this system within the marriage.* (The reflection process.)

"This is quite a re-think," said Mrs Anderson. "I have a feeling 125 that this interview will be entirely different from the interview that Jack expects, that the student expects, that Lorna expects."

However, in the earlier seminar, when we were working only on this 126 case, a lot of the steps were re-traced and the anxiety in Jack that had got into the student—that Lorna would not have her husband back—was gone over again. At this point one member of the group started calling Jack by the name of the group member who had been the most persistent in getting the group on to the punishment theme. Plaintively this member asked, "Are you really talking about my marriage?" It happened a second time and what this confusion was about I never understood. "It's 'Jack'," roared the group in unison. "Well, I'd better shut up for a bit," said the misnamer. The discussion went back to the difficulty of handling a straight disagreement with one's co-worker when one was also supervising that worker. "But it might be to do with the case and the split getting into the workers," one member was able to remind the rest. Then Mrs Anderson confirmed the bit of this split that had got into her from her client in her emphasis of the separation needing to be total to give the couple time to think over their marriage. But this then left the student holding the other side—that they might need to confirm some things together with the help of their workers.

I attempted to close this part of the seminar to move on to another 127 case. "Well, we'll leave you with it," I said, "as we always do."

"Well," said Mrs Anderson, "interesting to see if I could get an 128 invitation out of my student to join him."

I supported this, saying that her going could be very important for 129 Lorna. She knew that Mrs Anderson had not intended to go, and she might now see that Mrs Anderson could go to an interview when at one time she had not wanted to do so. "For her and Jack it is difficult for them to have any conception that a disagreement does not have to mean total separation. If you and the student could get yourselves out of this bit of your fix and be seen to have resolved this difference, this either/or, then perhaps the clients would have a chance to do this too."

COMMENT

This example, given in some detail, shows where the group got stuck, when it was having a real struggle, and when it was able to move on in the discussion. There is, of course, a lot in the presented material which was not discussed in detail. Further discussion on the actual case would have been interesting and perhaps helpful to Mrs Anderson in her on-going work. But we were concerned with the supervision of the student and the particular problem in the work and the supervision at that point in time. Some work had to be done on the case so that the members, including the newcomers, could move as a group into thinking about the detailed problem. With a few false starts and several attempts to avoid the task, they were able to do this. The behaviour of the group is probably fairly typical of any group struggling with a new piece of difficult learning.

I will now comment on a few points which illustrate the main thesis and basic assumptions I outlined in the previous chapters.

In this presentation Mrs Anderson showed very clearly that she is able to work consciously with the transference and is not afraid of her own countertransference. With her, clients have a chance of getting "warmer" and therefore of being helped. She is prepared to get well into the situation, even if it gets a bit prickly at times, as it had done in this case and as it did in the seminar for her. She was quite clear about her identification with Lorna (par. 66) and the warmth and strength of the relationship was apparent in the things she had taken up with her and in Lorna's subsequent response (pars. 36 and 55). She is experienced enough not to have to walk into every trap that is set for her. She had not responded to the enormous pressure Lorna puts on people to treat her like a little girl (pars. 56–58).

But at the end of her very vivid description of Jack and Lorna she showed that she was not afraid of exposing the trap into which she had recently walked and out of which she could not get herself. Just because of her closeness to Lorna's dissociated anxiety, which she was not able to pick up consciously, she identified with the defence-against-anxiety utilised by Lorna (see pages 44–46). In this case, she reflected Lorna's defence particularly clearly, not only because of her own work with Lorna, but because Mr Clark's reflection of Jack in the supervision was strong enough to force her into the opposite role (see page 45). She reacted *against* his over-statement, rather than *with* it (see page 44), and this compounded her already existing identification with Lorna. The pressure came from two directions—from her own client and from the student.

The anxiety which Jack expressed about the changed situation which so clearly got into the student was also, I think, in Lorna. She was much more anxious about her new state of freedom and the future of her marriage and the way she was now punishing Jack than she dared to know. This girl has obviously got very real strengths which, because of her confusion about her sexual identity and conflict about whether to retreat into the position of being a little girl, get misused in a relationship with a member of the opposite sex. And I think it was this anxiety which was touched off in Mrs Anderson—her own doubts about her strength as a personality and as a worker, and whether she would misuse this (par. 120). And in over-defending herself against this fear, her countertransference being *with* her client and *against* that of her student, she reflected Lorna's outward attitude to Jack and in doing so indirectly punished Mr Clark by withdrawing her strength and failing to keep up the argument with him (her co-worker) in a way that could resolve it (a very real difficulty when the co-worker is also a student). By getting stuck in this situation, Mrs Anderson and Mr Clark offered an unfortunate model to the clients, which, if maintained, would have reinforced their defences guarding the anxiety about change and resolving differences. But, if they, the workers, could get out of this, the clients would, in the long run, be better off when presented with the workers' resolution than if their workers had never been involved enough with their own clients to get into this difficulty (see page 41).

It is very noticeable in the seminar that Mrs Anderson is confident and flexible enough to be able to recognise and acknowledge her own collusion. No seminar of this type ever asks a member to take the advice of the group or to relinquish the responsibility for what they choose to do (par 127). But Mrs Anderson gave up her defence and shifted her stance surprisingly rapidly—from the feeling that it would be a very destructive interview (par. 88), first to Jack (par. 92), then to Mr Clark (par. 100), then to being able to comment on his strengths in the situation (par. 103), then to wondering whether she might get an invitation out of him (par. 128), and finally to getting excited about the forthcoming interview, saying, "I think that this interview will be entirely different from the interview that Jack expects, that the student expects, that Lorna expects." (par. 125)

This was probably because her own anxiety was very near to consciousness and she was well aware that her defence and immediate work with the student were not satisfactory. This was apparent in her presentation. After the clarity of her account of the case and of some of her previous work, she presented her immediate confusion and difficulty, both in her words and in her change of manner (pars. 22–23). She half-knew that she was leaving Mr Clark to sink or swim on his own inappropriately in this case. This got confused with another issue, the autonomy of the probation officer, which failed to solve it, because it was irrelevant to the way she had chosen to work this particular case and irrelevant to the dynamics of the case itself which had got into the two workers. This sort of difficulty cannot be solved on a principle of that kind, but only, I think, through understanding a little more about the interaction in a particular situation. So she was, despite her arguments for autonomy, left with the muddle and dissatisfaction which were somewhere connected with punishing or the misuse of strength— "... all muddled up with Jack's needs and Lorna's needs and the student's need ... and you don't punish your wife when you give her a baby." She "threw" this at the group. At first the other members turned away from this (par. 24), but then were able to come back to it, particularly when Mrs Anderson showed that she was quite prepared to discuss her fears about the forthcoming interview. Finally someone was able to ask her why she had allowed herself to get pushed out.

Although I did not do it consciously at the time, I think I must have picked up unconsciously that in her reflecting Lorna so strongly, and by withdrawing her own strength, Mrs Anderson was sometimes afraid of misusing her ability. But I can remember being quite vociferous and leaning towards her when I said it was *her* skill, not the student's, that I would back in what could be a most important and strategic interview (par. 119). Somehow I felt it necessary to undermine her doubts about her ability.

Mrs Anderson has reason to be confident about a lot of her casework. No doubt, like most averagely good caseworkers, she will do better work with some clients than with others. But in par. 110 she expressed less confidence about supervising. And she also did this by presenting the details of the case before stating her problem in the supervision. Another supervisor, more confident of her supervision and less confident about the work done previously on the case, might have presented it the other way round and said, "I'm worried and feel uncomfortable about letting my student do an interview he's determined to do. I can't resolve the argument with him and I now think I am leaving him in the lurch."

I do not think it matters which way round the presentation is made. Both the case and the supervision need to be looked at and brought together (which is why we often need two sessions to be able to see the reflection). The two examples in the introductory chapter were presented in different ways, one supervisor starting off by saying, "I feel like a wasp with my student", and the other supervisor starting off by describing his concern about the student's ability to handle a difficult case and then feeling he had mis-allocated it, because of the mutual difficulty in the supervision session of making some sense of the confusion and muddle. It is probably something to do with the nature of the case as well as the confidence of the supervisor, both in his work and in the group to whom he is presenting the work, which determines how the problem is stated. Probably, for people less experienced in this way of working, it is easier first to present the case followed by the supervision which has gone awry, rather than saying, "This is where I have gone awry, but I don't know what is causing it—this is the background."

What is noticeable in the description of the work with Jack and Lorna is that the student's reflection of Jack is much more wholesale than Mrs Anderson's of Lorna. Mr Clark illustrates the first manifestation of the reflection process which I described in chapter three (page 44) to such an extent that the two university tutors in the group could not believe we were discussing a student whom they both knew. Mrs Anderson's reflection of Lorna was much more circumscribed and depicted one aspect of the latter's anxiety and defence against that anxiety. Her manner of presenting the work changed radically when she came to this aspect and where it interfered with her own performance in the supervision. Her work illustrated the second manifestation of a reflection process (page 45) which I described, when the worker is not overall seduced into an open identification, but is so confused as to what is going on at a particular point in time that he portrays some aspects of the client's behaviour. That the student's reflection is often more general and that of the experienced worker more detailed, but sometimes more intensive on that one aspect, does not seem to me unexpected or surprising.

It is, of course, to Mr Clark's credit—and in the seminar when we heard a bit more about his other work he sounded potentially a very good worker—that he could allow himself to become identified with Jack and that he was so persistent with Mrs Anderson about his having an interview with Jack and Lorna together. As a student he had made a good start, had put his heart into his work and had gone into a generalised countertransference. With increasing experience his reflection of his clients will become more localised and more diagnostically useful. He can only do this after intensive experience with many cases. But, potentially, unless his job precludes him from developing his skills, he has the makings of a good caseworker. Although I have never met him and would not recognise him, and do not know his name, he has endeared himself to me. He was prepared to get into the marital problem while he had a chance, he felt and expressed very deep empathy for his client and he battled on against his supervisor's countertransference. I think Jack, inarticulate, as we learned, and probably unable to say it for himself, had a lot for which to thank Mr Clark.

Postscript

"We went up to the camp and it was a small room, not very convenient, and a rectangular table set against the wall. So I took the narrow end of the table and decided to let the rest of them sit where they would. Lorna came and sat on my left, as close to me as possible, and, incidentally, she put on her most attractive clothes—she really looked a dolly. I saw Jack waiting for us, obviously terribly anxious as to whether we were all coming or whether he was going to be let down. He was delighted to see us all pile out of the car and go into the shed. Without waiting to be called, he presented himself at the gate, and said, 'My Probation Officer's come to see me.' He came in and sat down, taking up the whole side of the table, but somehow we got ourselves balanced with Mr Clark and me at the ends of the table.

"You remember that at the seminar we talked about their inability to talk and Lorna's saying she was going to shame him. And on the way she said this again; it was about time Jack learned the truth. He was always accusing her of not being very good in bed. And she said, 'I'm going to tell Mr Clark what he does. I'm going to tell him in front of you and that'll make him be ashamed.' And, although I longed to say, 'Look, that's a dreadful thing to say to the man,' I thought, 'Well, I really must put this to the test and let her say it if that's what she wants, and perhaps pick up the pieces afterwards.' And she said how she was going to tell that when they had intercourse, Jack always masturbated afterwards, and she felt this was the most insulting thing that could happen, and that no woman would put up with it.

"So, we went up there and we talked. At first we talked about this non-communication, and Mr Clark made some very good interventions in that even hitting Lorna was a bit of communication, and this got Jack into looking at the number of times he'd hit Lorna in the past. And eventually, when we'd spoken very quietly for a while, Jack said, 'Well, come on then, what do you want to tell me about? We're supposed to be talking about things, what do you want to say to me?' And I thought, Well, here comes the crunch. There was a little bit of silence, and then Lorna said, 'I want to talk about babies.' So Jack said, 'Well, what about babies?' So she said, 'I don't want any more babies, and you know this is why I'm not good in bed,' which was interesting, because all her feelings for him were really in that sentence —you know, 'Forgive me, this is the reason.'

"And so we talked about being on the pill, which he'd always forbidden before, and we talked fairly light-heartedly about how he felt about this. But he felt that he could not accept not having more babies, but he was also trying to say, 'Look, I'll be more gentle as a lover.'

"And then we talked about his mother who's been such a bone of contention. Lorna decided she wanted to talk about his mother; whenever he wanted anything at all he went to Mum and she gave it to him. So then Jack decided, 'All right.' If Lorna didn't like his Mum, his Mum was out, he'd never write to her again, he'd never see her again and he didn't know what all the fuss was about. And Mr Clark was very sensible. He would not allow it to be dealt with in this manner. I can't quite remember what he said, but something like . . . when you marry you take on and make a new family, and that people in the new marriage have to give up a family, that Lorna had given up her family because of Jack and perhaps Jack could give up his family because of Lorna. And Jack could see that.

"That's about as much of the interview as I can remember, but when we drove back Lorna was happy the interview had gone so well and, although she wouldn't admit it, she had been dreading it. But she said, 'You needn't expect me to say that I'm going to have him back immediately, because I want to think about it. And when I visit him next time, I'll tell him.'

"Mr Clark was still very anxious, but in the supervisory session we went through what we thought had been accomplished—how, without coercion Lorna had been able to turn turtle and say, 'Forgive me for not being a good wife,' and the rest. Then very soon after that Lorna wrote, and Jack painfully wrote a letter of thanks to me for looking after Lorna, which I thought was interesting."

The rest of Mrs Anderson's account covered the developments in this case during the next year. They are not strictly relevant to the subject of this monograph. Mr Clark had left and Mrs Anderson continued to work with both Jack and Lorna on her own. But the interaction between this couple is so very interesting that I am including a summarised version of the rest of Mrs Anderson's account in an appendix. The work with Jack, done intensively for a short period by Mr Clark, and then subsequently by Mrs Anderson, gave him sufficient boost for him not to have to carry the badness for them both. It then became clearer how Lorna provoked him and how, with a husband working and with herself on the pill (apparently what she had previously wanted), she still has a lot of difficulties regarding her own sexuality and her own anger.

Summary

An experienced probation officer, Mrs Anderson, gave a very vivid summary of a case in which she was working with the wife, Lorna, and the student, Mr Clark, was working with the husband, Jack. Lorna was on probation and Jack was in prison. At the end of her presentation, Mrs Anderson lost her clarity and ended on a note of confusion about punishment.

Mr Clark was trying to get Lorna to the prison for a joint interview which he wished to conduct on his own, distrusting Mrs Anderson's attitude of not wanting to try to persuade Lorna into going for this interview, or into a reconciliation. Lorna was leaving her husband to "stew", refusing to say whether she would have him back or not. This prison sentence was different from previous ones when Lorna had been kept safe with a pregnancy; this time she had got herself an abortion. Mr Clark strongly identified with Jack, reflecting his anxiety about separation and about what Lorna might be up to on her own, and wanted to effect a reconciliation.

The Student's Reflection.

Mrs Anderson was loth to stop Mr Clark from holding this interview, believing in the autonomy of the probation officer, but she was worried that he might be out of his depth when faced with the highly verbal Lorna and the much less articulate Jack. The supervision had got stuck at this point; *either* the student held this interview which, as a threesome, the group thought could be destructive or a non-event; *or* there should not be an interview. Mrs Anderson and Mr Clark had not been able to resolve their argument. The interview was scheduled and Mrs Anderson was not in agreement with it being held, and worried about its outcome.

The Supervisor's Reflection.

The group was concerned that Mrs Anderson was punishing her student and leaving him in the lurch, as Lorna was punishing her husband and leaving him in the lurch. This was not typical of her usual supervisory behaviour. It took some time for the group to dare to look at this and they could do this only after they had explored the homosexual aspects of the interaction in the case in which the punishment of the opposite sex was manifest.

Mrs Anderson's continued concern about this interview and her presentation of the problem in the supervision indicated that the feelings behind the punishment of the student were very near to consciousness. But her initial defence of her stance was accentuated because of the reflection she carried in two ways; firstly, her student's reflection of Jack's anxiety about losing Lorna and of the changed situation when she was no longer safe with a baby, left her holding the doubts about a confrontation and the anxiety of what a reconciliation might mean in terms of further change; secondly, she carried the reflection from her own work with Lorna, who was much more anxious than she dared to know about in her new state of freedom. Lorna had great strengths which she, because of her confusion about her sexual identity, misused, and of which she was afraid, often retreating into the position of a little girl. This touched off Mrs Anderson's fears of her own strength of personality and as a worker; afraid of over-controlling her student, she "flogged" the argument of the autonomy of the worker, leaving him to manage this interview on his own, forgetting that she had previously opted to share the case, a situation in which neither worker has autonomy.

But this was so near to consciousness that when it was looked at in terms of the pressure from the case and through the student's reflection of Jack, she was able to relinquish her own reflection of the defence very quickly and start to think how she could get an invitation out of her student to join the interview, a course obviously much more appropriate when the case is being worked by two workers. It no longer had to be an either/or situation, the student holding it on his own, or her forbidding it. This type of argument was very typical of the clients. Instead it became possible for her to envisage offering the clients a new model that she and Mr Clark could work together despite a disagreement, and she could show Lorna that she could go to an interview of which she had previously disapproved. If Mrs Anderson and Mr Clark could resolve their countertransference which had got into their argument, and could be seen to do this, then the clients might have a chance of resolving some of their either/or arguments. The clients were unlikely to be able to do this, if the workers were still fighting in the same vein.

The Group's Reflection. The group were relatively experienced at looking at the interaction in a case, but, even so, the discussion at one point got stuck on whether it was Lorna punishing Jack, or Jack punishing Lorna, when it was evident that each had been doing their equal share.

This example also illustrated the additional difficulty of supervising one's co-worker.

Example II

THE PROBLEM OF BELONGING

This example shows a much subtler reflection, much less near to consciousness on the part of the supervisor and of the student. As in the previous example, the supervisor shared the case with the student, and this emphasised the reflection in the supervision process. This is coincidence. In fact, we worked on many more cases in which the supervisor was not an active worker.

I have chosen this example, because it is about the whole question of involvement and depicts a student who explicitly propounded her fears of getting involved in a piece of work without a legal mandate. The student's sense of justice ostensibly prevented her from holding the client. "Have I the right to 'pry'? Have I the right to interfere?" are the questions commonly asked by students, which could be translated, "Do I dare to get closer?" The fear behind these questions is accentuated when the time-span of the placement is limited and the students' own fears about separation after involvement are activated. It is appropriate for anyone, who has limited experience and limited confidence in their own ability to be helpful, to be tentative. Anyone with a sense of responsibility is likely to be scared. But why does this problem become so much more of a difficulty with some cases than with others? This, I think, is sometimes to do with the case and the reflection from that case compounds the student's problem; the problem is not totally his. (For all I know, Mr Clark may have had some difficulty in getting closer to some of his clients, but with the case of Jack and Lorna Hill, Jack would not let him "off the hook".) In this example the student had no difficulty in getting into the work; but she lost part of it, when she did not show a tendency to lose other cases.

This example also illustrates very clearly the importance of understanding something of the detail, rather than the overall fact, of the transference which is in operation.

The summary is on page 93.

THE CASE OF RODERICK AND CELIA FOSTER

Presenting:	Probation Officer:	Mr Gerald Knights
Worker:	Student:	Miss Elizabeth Regan; two-year graduate course
Family:	Husband:	Mr Roderick Foster, aged 27 ⎫ married
	Wife:	Mrs Celia Foster, aged 33 ⎭ five years
	Children:	Hazel Taylor, aged 16, child of Celia's first marriage

Betty Taylor, aged 13 ⎱ children of Celia's
Peter Taylor, aged 11 ⎰ second "marriage",
                      i.e. cohabitation
Jonathan Taylor, aged 8, child of Celia's
third "marriage"
Jenny Foster, aged 2, child of present
marriage

Mr Knights, like Mrs Anderson, is an experienced probation officer.   1
Benign, and with an innate courtesy, he is a great sticker-with-the-
problem in his casework, in his supervision of students, and in a
working group. Speaking thoughtfully and with a slight hesitation in
his voice, he has often been the one who has brought the group back
from a flight from the task.

Just over a year ago, Roderick had been placed on probation, pre-   2
viously having had a clean record. But Roderick and Celia had been
known to the probation department in another connection for some time.*

Roderick, a man of average intelligence, had been an adopted child   3
of parents who were middle-aged at the time of adoption. He had
one sister, an adult when he was a child, who might have been his
natural mother. When he was young he was very close to his father,
and his mother seems to have been very much in the background. But
when he was sixteen, his father relinquished the reins to his mother,
started to fade out and then died when Roderick was twenty.

Celia never knew her father and was brought up by her mother and   4
stepfather in a rigid and Victorian atmosphere. She had one half-
sister who was mentally handicapped. At seventeen she became pregnant and "had to marry" the father of Hazel, but they agreed to part
after one year. She referred to her second and third partners as "husbands", one of whom had had a criminal record. It was not known why
she had separated from these men.

Roderick and Celia had felt their marriage to be a love-match, but   5
the year before his offence he had had a casual affair and eight months
later he still felt guilty about this and the marriage was felt to be in a
crisis. They parted and Roderick went to the Midlands. Celia had an
affair "to pay Roderick back", but did not enjoy it. When Roderick
came to Court, Celia took him back. At the time the order was made,
there was an accommodation problem, there were debts, and Roderick
was very angry and feeling that everyone was being vindictive to him.

Mr Knights had tried to focus the work on the marriage, but in-   6
creasingly Celia had withdrawn from him and, at the time he presented
this case, Roderick was making less frequent contact. However, many
of the problems had been resolved. They had obtained a council house,

---

* The detail of this and of the charge is purposely not specified.

the debts had been cleared, and materially everything was running smoothly. Yet Roderick was still guilty about his affair and it was very unclear what was happening in the marriage. And it had recently emerged that Celia and a friends of hers, also well known to the probation department, had been on shoplifting sprees in another town. She had been caught and charged, but the Court had not insisted on her attendance and, in her absence, she had been fined. At this time, Hazel, who previously had always lived with her maternal grandmother and had had a Victorian upbringing similar to that of her mother, was brought into the family and soon after this committed a shoplifting offence. A supervision order was made and she became the client of Miss Elizabeth Regan who had just started a placement with Mr Knights. Miss Regan made a very good contact with Hazel, and also with Celia, but as these relationships started to gain life, Roderick became much more elusive and Mr Knights was having difficulty in holding on to him. And then, a few weeks before this presentation, Celia was charged with another offence in the town in which they lived and was due to appear in the local Court the following week. Miss Regan was not sure at all whether she would recommend a probation order.

This series of seminars was taking place during a power shortage 7 and the first part of Mr Knights' presentation was not recorded. When the power came on Mr Knights was saying, "My difficulty in presenting this case is, I think, that it is so involved, there seem to be so many facets to it. So I hope everyone is understanding me, but I haven't yet told you about Elizabeth.

"Well, she is in her early twenties and she's really an exciting person 8 to have around the office. She's bright, she is quick to grasp the material, and she is very liberal in her approach. And, as I said, with a girl like Hazel she is able right away to make good contact. I got an enormous satisfaction from the interview she had with her on . . . her second day, I think, at the office.

"I might say, that at the time when I heard that Elizabeth was 9 coming to me and without knowing that Hazel was coming before the Court, I had considered the idea of putting her in touch with Celia and seeing how this worked out. But then Hazel got into trouble and Elizabeth came in on the crisis of this offence. And then other things happening since—Celia now coming before the Court—my fear is that *I have loaded the poor girl too much* with very important things that are going on in this case. And I have the suspicion that *I am being unfair to Elizabeth* in giving her this work to do while I hang on to Roderick. Later on your comments on this would be very helpful. (N.B. the weight of feeling that is reflected.)

"The first thing that became clear was that after her interview with 10

Hazel, which went off very successfully, she met Celia. And what was important, I think, was that Celia wasn't really the 'hard' (in inverted commas) person that Roderick had been trying to make out to me that she was; that inside Celia was longing for the opportunity of having her own worker and gladly responded to Elizabeth's invitation to talk. What came out was that Celia was very much regarding herself as on the same basis as Hazel, in that Hazel had gone through the same experience of Victorian upbringing with a rigid mother that she had had, in a little village miles from anywhere, and therefore felt a great bond of sympathy between her daughter and herself. And I thought, if Celia can respond to Elizabeth in this way and bring up these conflicts, then, perhaps, this would rub off on the marriage.

"Another strand to this is Celia's great depression and discomfort 11 about Roderick's adultery which is now over two years old, and the fact that it is still worrying her very considerably. And she is puzzled by it. At the same time she is saying, 'Well, Roderick has changed considerably. He is now what I consider to be an ideal husband, but I find I can't respond to this.' This is the point Elizabeth has reached with her. What Elizabeth and I were discussing in our session last week was, really is it a question of Celia putting her own fears about herself into Roderick and feeling that she can't respond to him? And this is the sort of line that Elizabeth is going to follow."

The discussion settled on three areas. Firstly, whether Elizabeth 12 was likely to recommend a probation order for Celia. "Flirting with the probation service" was the expression that was eventually used when it was noted how until recently she had not been in trouble herself, not until Roderick had had some help from Mr Knights. But she had had three husbands out of the four who had been in trouble and over several years had had an "in and out" relationship with many probation officers in her other connection with the department. "We all knew her," said Mr Knights. "It was almost as if she had a need to be courted by the probation service," said another member, who worked in the same office. "But then she started shoplifting." And we learnt that through a series of administrative errors, Mr Knights' report to the other Court had not been accepted, and she had got a fine. Could Elizabeth be helped to see her need not to be allowed to go on flirting —to try and really get hold of her by recommending a probation order. Something in this woman was asking to be taken hold of—she seemed to be asking for help and trying to get more attached to the service. Perhaps Elizabeth had more chance to do this than Mr Knights or all the other workers who had known her.

Secondly, the discussion moved to Celia's relationship with Hazel. 13 The more Mr Knights talked about it, the more intertwined and symbiotic it sounded. "Sisterly" was the word Celia used when describing her extreme fellow-feeling for Hazel. It was not clear why Hazel had suddenly been imported into the family after Celia had been fined in the other Court. And then she had immediately got herself on a supervision order. This kept Celia in touch with the service. How much was Hazel's offence unconsciously on behalf of Celia? She had got the officer Celia might have got after her offence. What was Celia projecting into Hazel, or was she even consciously putting her up to it? "If Hazel becomes the bad one, can she now enjoy her marriage again?"

"This is my fear," said Mr Knights.   14

And thirdly, we discussed what we came to call the *belonging* in   15
this case. "What, Gerry, was your reason, or intuition, or your feeling when you first said that you think if Celia at last gets her own worker, that Roderick might not be able to take it? You said you thought he might commit another offence."

"I think Roderick might commit another offence, because originally   16
he was the focal point in this family. He was the reason for having helpers in and out. But now he's got a daughter from beyond. Another daughter suddenly comes into the family and immediately gets a supervising officer. In addition to this his wife looks as if she'll get a supervising officer. Everybody seems to be moving over to their side."

"So the only way for him to get in again may be for him to go and do   17
a 'job', isn't it?"

"I wonder if this is quite the right emphasis," I intervened. "Both   18
Celia and Roderick seemed to have had only one parent. Celia never knew her father. We don't know anything about her relationship with her step-father, but we do know that her half-sister was mentally handicapped and presumably took additional time and attention. Roderick's adoptive father was predominant through his earlier childhood and then suddenly seemed to fade away when he was sixteen, his adoptive mother coming to the fore and taking over, but he still does not know whether his sister was his natural mother, and, like Celia, he never knew his real father. I wonder if this couple cannot let themselves have two parents. Or is it whether they can't bear to share a parent-figure? Gerry couldn't get hold of Celia and, as well as her only flirting with the service, it may be that Roderick had to keep her out of the work and have Gerry for himself."

"So what's going to happen when Elizabeth's placement ends? Will   19
you, Gerry, be having all three of them?"

"No, I think having got two officers in it now, I might try and get   20
another colleague to share the case with me."

"But I am not clear what is happening in the marriage. Roderick says   21
the marriage is better and he is better, but the delinquency is worse."

"Hazel's arrival seems to have had the effect of averting the ₁ocus   22
from the marriage."

"What did Roderick see in Celia when he married her? Here was a   23
woman who had had three marriage failures and already had four
children."

"And what was his reaction to acquiring suddenly a sixteen-year old   24
daughter?"

"His immediate reaction was, 'Let's have the whole family together,   25
and it doesn't matter whether it's my child or Celia's.' "

"His real reaction?"   26

"Well, he certainly didn't give me any indication that he dislikes it."   27

"Could we get a bit closer to this," I said. "Roderick and Celia   28
made it very clear they were in love—they felt they had found something very important for their inner worlds. Presumably they shared
some unconscious fantasy which was part of the attraction.[2] And
importing the sixteen-year old seems to be important to both of them.
I wonder if the two are connected. The discussion seems to be hovering
around these two things."

"Is Hazel being used to help them solve what they were trying to   29
solve and get in touch with when they first married, which hasn't
quite come off?"

"Celia must be worried about being a sort of female Henry VIII. To   30
have three husbands, perhaps, is permissible; to have four is a bit
getting out on a limb. To have five? Perhaps there is a lot of talk about
a happy marriage which doesn't exist. Perhaps they can't bear to admit
that this marriage is going to be a failure."

"Perhaps they feel they can't exist as a unit on their own. Because   31
they used to have his adoptive mother living with them, didn't they?"

"There's something about the advent of Hazel at sixteen. She comes   32
across so much like her mother. It's almost as if you've got two Celias.
I wonder if Elizabeth feels the same, that she's dealing with one person."

Then the discussion suddenly became extreme in its tone and ex-   33
aggerated beyond the facts we had been given. Celia was described as
the woman who had cast off three husbands and, now married to a
man six years younger, had "a child on the loose", "a husband on the
loose", and "was now doing her share of the looting". The marriage
was seen as an "abysmal failure".

Apparently at the time I did not take this up and I cannot now   34
remember whether I put up a conscious check in my mind to intervene if it went on much longer. But a member of the group indirectly
related to the exaggeration that was being expressed—an exaggeration
often typical of the expression of the swings of emotion in adolescence.
"Somehow," she said, "I've got stuck in the adolescence of Roderick
and Celia, and with the advent of Hazel I'm stuck even more. Because
with Roderick you have the confusion of his teens when his parents
changed their roles and the confusion about his sister. And Celia had a

strict upbringing and then conceived a baby before marriage when she was sixteen or seventeen. I think both of them had great difficulty at that age."

There was a pause and I decided to take on this theme. "Yes," I 35 said, "I think adolescence is terribly important in this case. I have been thinking that the age at which Hazel is brought into the family is the same age that Celia must have been when she had or conceived her. I wonder if Hazel keeps Roderick and Celia in touch with their own problem, whether they feel she can solve something for them that they can't solve together. Last August it seemed as if they were keeping up a facade or a pretence that things were all right when materially they had been able to get things straighter, but then the work seemed to become less dynamic. It felt as if the work had got a bit stuck then, and, may be, this was because they could not share Gerry. It seems fortunate that Elizabeth has come into the case, because I wonder if the shared internal fantasy[3] is about sisters. It must have been difficult for Celia having a mentally handicapped half-sister, and Roderick was and is confused about whether his sister is really his mother. Did Roderick marry the older woman with several children to maintain the confusion whether important women are elder sisters? Neither of them can get over a casual affair, now over two years old. Does this connect back to what they feel about their own births? Does this connect with anything they are saying, Gerry?"

"Yes, it does ring a bell. Roderick and Celia's main fear is that 36 Hazel will meet a boy and become pregnant. And a lot of discussion has gone on between me and Roderick about this sort of thing. He feels that if he is bringing up children they should be allowed to speak out about sex, and sex must be dealt with above board. Then he shakes his fist and says, 'One thing they mustn't do, they mustn't bring any trouble to this house,' meaning they mustn't come in pregnant."

"How is Elizabeth being used? As a sister?" 37

"Perhaps, I'm not sure. Perhaps like an older sister. But Roderick 38 has kept only one appointment with me since Elizabeth arrived. Then he saw me the day of the Court appearance and then he missed his appointment this week."

"What does he think of Elizabeth?" 39

"Welcomes her into the family with open arms." 40

"Why? I would expect him not to be so keen." 41

"Well, he feels he can't communicate with Hazel, and by implication 42 with Celia. And more by implication, when he sees Elizabeth being able to communicate with Hazel, he's . . . very grateful."

"At the beginning of the morning he seemed a very important person. 43 Now it's all Celia and Hazel."

"And we've never talked of the four other children. What about the 44
two-year old? She is the one joint child they really share."

"We don't even know if he loves the baby." 45

"Perhaps this is not so surprising. If we're right and the problem 46
is more to do with an adolescent age, the two-year old may feel very
safe. All their psychic energy may be converging on what happens
when children are sixteen. But it does seem very important that the
work is now done with Celia and Hazel and Roderick, or else Betty
and Peter, and . . . Jonathon, is it, may well be in trouble when they
get to sixteen. This seems a very crucial age for this family. Are things
re-enacted for them and get stirred up when the child gets to this age?"

"It's only the two-year old who's got a complete couple of parents. 47
Roderick, Celia, Hazel, Betty, Peter and Jonathon are all steps or
adopted. An awful lot of parents haven't stuck."

"Elizabeth's got a terrific chance going in on this case at her age, 48
but she's not going to stick."

"She hasn't got long. If it's possible, I wonder whether there is 49
enough time to work to help Celia with her own identity. I think this
is fundamental."

"To help her to separate from Hazel. If she was a bit clearer about 50
her own identity, she might not use Hazel so much to express the
problem. What do you think, Gerry?"

"Can you sort of detail that one for me?" 51

"I'd hate to try. There are so many bits and pieces in this jigsaw. 52
But Celia doesn't identify much with her Victorian upbringing, although she left Hazel there to have the same thing, and she never
knew her own father. And she must feel so unlovable having lost three
husbands. If Elizabeth could help her to sort out her feelings about all
these things, she might not have to remain so identified with the sixteen-
year old."

"She's only got three months." 53

"Would it be a bit more possible," I said, "for Elizabeth to do some- 54
thing, if we didn't think of her doing too much. I think this connects
back to what you were saying at the beginning, Gerry, that you felt
you were clobbering Elizabeth with too much—with two bodies. But
there are lots of cases where one has two clients, and in view of what
we have been discussing, it doesn't seem extraordinary that Celia found
her way to Elizabeth via Hazel. Is the feeling of clobbering, or having
too much to do, connected with the weight of emotion in the case?
And are we expressing this now by too high an expectation, not only
because you feel Elizabeth is such a good student, but also from what's
in the case—that adolescent expectations are very high. Roderick
and Celia had high expectations from being in love. They have found
it terribly difficult to admit the difficulties between them. It all gets put

on to an affair as the cause of the difficulty. Is it too high an expectation that Elizabeth could, in the time, do much along this line? It seems a very big job for anyone to attempt in that space of time. It's a bit like what we were talking about yesterday—that it would take years to work with the basic deprivation of Mr and Mrs O. (the case which my colleague and I had presented at a plenary session) and their missing parent, but that we might do something which would make life more comfortable for them by helping them to give up the unrealistic ideal, being a bit more accepting of what they had got, both the strengths and the weaknesses, rather than trying to make up to them twenty years later what they never had. Not only is it too broad a focus and too large and distant to see the end, but it makes, by being too big, success less possible. As you said in the beginning, 'Poor Elizabeth'. It feels too much. What can Elizabeth do? Can we think not in terms of Elizabeth helping Celia to grow up overnight, but in terms of helping to shift where they are stuck at the moment. What is Celia saying?"

"It came out so clearly in my session with Elizabeth last week that   55
Celia's great fear at present—what is most crippling to her—is the great worry about Roderick's adultery. Of course one's going to be upset about this, but with Celia this has gone on so long that there seems more to it than this. Could Elizabeth relate the adultery back to the sort of image Celia has of herself."

"Ummmm." (That was my Um. I was still thinking that we wanted   56
to get into the detail—the actual fantasy or feeling behind this difficulty.) "Could we think what the meaning of the adultery is, when, other things getting better, he remains so guilty and she so unforgiving after two years. Apart from the social meaning of adultery, what might the inner meaning to these two be?"

"To Celia it must mean the threat of the loss of a fourth husband.   57
She's lost three husbands already, and this one means much more to her. Adultery is one means of losing your husband. She may have thought he preferred someone else. He must be guilty at giving her these feelings."

"I think this may be related to Celia's feelings that she is unlovable."   58
"Is that what the shoplifting is about?"   59
"I wonder, Gerry, whether to generalise it in terms of 'Am I lov-   60
able?' is too vague. Loving means different things to different people. I wonder if with this couple being in love is something about belonging. Roderick has expressed great doubts about whom he belonged to. Was his sister his mother? And I imagine that many adopted children do have feelings about where they really belong. And Celia may have had very big doubts how much she belonged with her step-father and having to compete with the probable extra attention given to a handi-capped sister. Might the extended feelings about the adultery be about

having something which doesn't belong, or raise the doubt whether they belong to each other? And is the shoplifting about having something which doesn't really belong? Roderick says his adultery was very casual and Celia said that her adulterous response to pay him out meant nothing to her. But both of them say this still gets between them. I may be wrong, but I have the feeling that the accentuated response to the adultery may mean, 'does the other belong to someone else?' "

"In a way this has reminded me, a link in my own mind, with 61 Roderick's saying that Celia is independent. He once said, 'She doesn't fully *belong* to me, she can stand on her own two feet. I'm not crucial to her ability to cope.' He said, 'If I die tomorrow, she'd get on all right.' "

"I can't go along with belonging being different from loving. If 62 belonging is different from loving, I would like to be told how."

There followed what was quite a squabble as to whether the idea 63 of belonging was useful in relation to this case, or whether we were just having a semantic argument. Some thought belonging was a more primitive form of loving, and argued whether one could love the other person if they did not belong to you. Did Celia feel that Hazel belonged to her when she expressed so much identification with her? Could you start to share if loving meant just whether you belonged or not? "Very difficult to relate if all your energy's going into just ensuring whether you belong or not."

"Do you think in their sense that loving is about exclusive property? 64 Do they see love as exclusive?"

"Belonging implies a very exclusive love . . . you know . . . you can't 65 let go. A more grown-up love is sharing, feeling safe in the sharing."

"Belonging seems a very passive notion. It's to do with other people 66 possessing in some way."

The discussion moved on to Roderick's relief that Hazel had some- 67 one to talk to. Did he identify with her coming into the family and starting to belong? Did he connect this with his concern about belonging?

The time was nearly up. "Could we move on," I said, "to the im- 68 plications of this in Gerry's work with Elizabeth. Is Gerry's having said at the beginning that he is clobbering Elizabeth with too much a way of saying that she is getting too much of the weight of belonging? Does this give us some indication of the strength of the unconscious fantasy in the marriage? Perhaps the work was fairly safe when Roderick just belonged to you, but explains a little why he and Celia couldn't let her come into the work. Now Celia has got someone else to belong to, if Elizabeth can get a probation order on her. You have said that Roderick welcomes Hazel having Elizabeth, but that he might commit another offence to get back to you. But I wonder if his feelings about

Hazel having Elizabeth are more mixed than he says, and whether *you carry for him the bit that is perhaps envious, or fears that belonging is too destructive, or too heavy for the other person to bear.* "Continuing to refer to this reflection, I went on,"Difficult . . . if this gets into the supervision and what goes on between you and Elizabeth. If he is also identifying with Hazel and her difficulties at sixteen—his difficulties at sixteen when his father started to fade out—it seems very important that you don't fade out."

"I don't jump on him when he misses one Tuesday evening."   69

"I'm not suggesting that you might lose him, but that Roderick   70
himself might see that he gets lost, just as he perceived losing his own father. So, in a sense, not only must you not get lost in your own right, but make sure that Roderick doesn't succeed in making it happen. But what about Elizabeth? If she gets a probation order on Celia, Celia will have a chance of belonging, rather than just flirting with the service. But Elizabeth is only going to be here for a few months."

"How long has she got?"   71

"Another three months."   72

"The feelings about belonging are now directed on Elizabeth."   73

"And on Hazel."   74

"Is Hazel the symbol of the extra-marital relationship, when they're   75
so worried about the old adultery?"

"Does Celia bring Hazel into the family at this time as someone who   76
doesn't belong to Roderick?"

"There's only eleven years difference in their ages. What if Roderick   77
commits adultery with Hazel? What if this gets acted-out?"

"Time is nearly up. Could we come back to someone's point that   78
Elizabeth is going to be here long enough to do some work, long enough to get involved—she already is. But with this thing about belonging, it is going to be difficult for Celia when she leaves, if this isn't worked with from the beginning. She'll need lots of time for the transfer."

"Is it important that Celia and Hazel share one supervising officer?   79
Can she help them to share her and be a bit more separate and then separate from her?"

"Yes, if Celia is saying they always feel the same thing."   80

"Can she help them to see themselves as more separate in relation to   81
her?"

"If they couldn't both belong to Gerry before, if they couldn't   82
share him, could Elizabeth work with her to get her to Gerry by the time she leaves?"

"She has been groping towards you for over a year . . . longer."   83

"Perhaps better to get back to only one worker. Use the period   84
with two of you to work on the feelings about belonging to get her to you, and you then work with the two of them on this."

The discussion went back over the earlier ground of Celia's long   85
flirtation with the service. Could Elizabeth get her to stick and help her
to Gerry when she left?

Again I said, "We have to stop. Can we have it back again in April,   86
Gerry?"

"Will the Court place her on probation?"   87

"What if Roderick commits incest?"   88

"Coffee."   89

TWO MONTHS LATER

Celia had been lost. The Court had given her a suspended sentence   90
and Elizabeth had not seen her since the Court hearing.

"I think we agreed last time that I was really asking Elizabeth to   91
undertake a very tough task—that whilst I was holding Roderick,
that I was asking her to carry both Hazel and Celia. Perhaps I can
jump off with two things. First, when I went back to my session with
Elizabeth, I gave her a rundown on what we had discussed, and I
gathered she was uncertain which way she was going to decide on the
case. She went back to see Celia again and we were to meet in four or
five days' time. But during this time Celia came into the office—and
this is the second thing—and this was a point of great significance for
Celia and Elizabeth, in that Celia started crying. And this had happened
in another of Elizabeth's cases when a man client had cried on her.
And this had really hit Elizabeth for six, because, she explained, she
doesn't know what to do. Her immediate reaction is to put her . . .
is to want to put her hand round the client's shoulder, but then she
draws back from this, because she thinks in some ways she is belittling
the client. But, anyway, from this interview with Celia she seemed to
take away Celia's need, and, indeed, Celia's wish, to come into the
office to see her. When we discussed the writing of the report, Elizabeth
said she wanted to recommend probation. I pointed out the difficulties
—that the Court might look at it in a more punitive way—but I said I
thought she had good reason for recommending probation, and that
it was her responsibility to put this as clearly and as concisely as she
could. And she's good at writing reports. She is able to express very
easily on paper what she feels and she can supply a very vivid picture.
In fact she wrote what I consider to have been a highly competent report, and the reader wouldn't have been left in any doubt. But, as you
heard, other things happened and Celia got a suspended sentence.

"But after this what worried Elizabeth most was the ethical part   92
of going and seeing Celia. Elizabeth didn't feel it was right or proper.
She felt very strongly that the proper way of going about it would be
to go to Celia and say, 'If you wish, I can come around every so often and
see you. Would you like me to do it?" Because of the tone in which she

said this, I said, 'Don't you think if you put it that way you are inviting Celia to say, No?''

"And this was extremely difficult. I felt myself getting a little more 93 rigid against her for taking this view. On the other hand her view could be upheld. I felt that after two or three sessions of talking on this one that she and I reached a compromise about it, and she did go and try and make appointments, but every time she went, Celia was missing. So in the end Celia was lost."

"Was she lost from the point of the crying?" 94

"Did Elizabeth feel she had lost her then?" 95

"I don't know, but certainly Elizabeth's response to the crying was 96 a lack of confidence in knowing how to handle it. Celia was very angry about the suspended sentence, and in both instances Elizabeth was very tentative in her approach—almost as if she didn't want to belittle Celia by holding on to the regret about not being on probation. It was too open-ended the way she offered to go and see her if she wanted . . . as though it didn't matter too much.

"You see, Elizabeth has a strong sense of justice. And there seems 97 to be a conflict between this and her doubts where to focus a case. And sometimes she accuses me of theorising too much. Do other people have these sort of accusations handed out to them? I have had the experience, you know, on several occasions of, 'Well, that's only theory, and that is only conjecture, and that is speculation,' which, in fact, is a pretty true assessment. But at least I try and look at it as some form of exploration. But there is resistance to this—the work needs to be all warmth, all humanity, and all support. I felt myself getting bogged down in my sessions with Elizabeth as to how I should overcome this one."

"But this, when it came to the point, is what she couldn't do. When 98 Celia cried and she had the emotion there in the room . . ."

"She feels that comforting is belittling, and then accuses you of 99 theorising."

"The problem of when do you use your feelings and when do you use 100 your head?"

"Or how do you bring the two together?" 101

"This seems to be the thing she is grappling with at the moment. 102 If she can't carry the two together, perhaps you are bound to get accused of one or the other."

"I should point out that she was accusing me in the nicest possible 103 way."

COMMENT
This was the final seminar of the year and during the last part of it, with continued reference to Miss Regan and other students whose cases

7

had been presented, we discussed more generally the difficulty of
students' integrating bits of theory into their practice. The supervisors
felt that the students got a "bellyfull" of theory at the university and that
they then got a reaction against this when the students were faced with
the multiple problems of their clients and the difficulty of facing with
the clients the pain in the work. The perennial problem of the students'
being afraid to overstep their role and "pry" into the affairs of the
clients was raised as was the confusion that several students, including
Miss Regan, expressed. With her the confusion became channelled on
where to focus the work. "And I have felt in myself," said Mr Knights,
"an urgency to provide a focus which she could argue against and have
her doubts. And this appeared to help. And then she would present more
confusion, and the more confusion she presented, the more urgency I
felt that *I* must help her more actively."

In this final discussion, when we were trying to bring some things
together, and, no doubt, expressing the difficulties of the group itself
with this type of learning, and getting confused and getting in a muddle,
I tried to stress three things which we could take away. The first concerned the confusion. It was not surprising that if the student was expressing confusion—her own and that in the cases—the supervisor
might be pushed into the role of non-confuser. (This is probably what was
happening to me at this moment. The supervisors were getting me to
feel what it was like to be them.) It did not seem inappropriate for the
supervisor to say (to himself), "I will hold on to a bit of firmness
against which you can be confused," or "I'll enter some of this confusion with you." Either of these ways seemed to be more appropriate
than leaving the student with it on his own. But I did not think we
should despise the confusion, as I was sure there could be no real
learning, particularly learning about emotional things, without considerable confusion and muddle *en route*. I doubted whether anyone
ever learnt anything difficult in this line if they could never afford to be
confused or muddled. It seemed to me that Miss Regan was really
working on what was important for her on this particular placement.

Secondly, I thought that it was too facile to expect much integration
of theory and practice on a basic course. In my experience, integrating
small bits of theory into one's practice took years, particularly the
psychological theory. Of all the theory they were given in the university,
they would hear and ponder on the bits that somewhere problematically
met their own internal world and at a point when they were able to
start to grapple with this. If they could throw one problem of this nature
at their supervisor, as Miss Regan was doing, they were properly
engaged on a real learning process.

And thirdly, as much as these were problems belonging to all students
and all workers, I thought we must not forget that they also belonged

to the clients. The workers were influenced by the clients. And Miss Regan's difficulties in hanging on to Celia when no probation order had been made, also belonged to Celia. It sounded as if a collusion had gone on. Miss Regan had her own doubts based on justice, but that she was able to ignore what had happened between her and Celia before the Court hearing was also something to do with Celia. Their mutual ambivalence had compounded Miss Regan's own doubts. We knew that Celia had "flirted" with the probation service for several years and never had really been able to "belong" and come in on the work. Perhaps Miss Regan was glad to get out of it, but this was not just her problem. Rather, it was a problem exemplified when client and worker both had doubts about the safety of getting closer and warmer.

The reader will note that the group lost the case, as Miss Regan had lost Celia. We never got round to enquiring about what was happening between Miss Regan and Hazel, and between Mr Knights and Roderick. Mr Knights insisted that he did not want a whole session for the "bring-back" of his case and we let him get away with this. He had to be pressed to bring it at all, and after his short report, both he and the group preferred to move on to the more general issues described above. But over many years I have never known Mr Knights to be a defaulter, or semi-defaulter, in this way. He had always shown himself to be a sticker-with-the-problem (par. 1). In this respect he was acting out of character, and it is in these instances that I believe the reflection process is relevant to the thinking. And it was this I was emphasizing in paras 54 and 68. With all his experience, he had as much difficulty in holding on to Roderick (par. 38) as Elizabeth did to Celia, and, in view of the clients' histories, I do not think this is surprising.

This recording of the group discussion shows that the group had moved quite a long way in being able to think associatively to the material which was given, despite the period when they "took-off" (par. 33), which was, I think, when the case really got into them and they reflected Roderick and Celia's exaggerated reaction to the adultery. But, if we were right in our understanding that the work had got stuck where an unconscious fantasy about who was the parent and who belonged to whom intruded strongly into the work (i.e. was there in the transference), it was likely, until this was noticed and understood, that Mr Knights and Miss Regan would reflect it in their behaviour together when thinking about the case. It was likely that Mr Knights would be worried that too much belonged to Miss Regan and that he himself was fading out. And it was likely that she, when it came to the crunch (and without an order) would lose Celia, not only because of her own difficulties of working with the pain of Celia's fantasy of never having really belonged, but also because of Celia's defence against the anxiety of belonging with which she unconsciously identified and which

she then reflected (see page 46). Both Mr Knights and Miss Regan identified with the clients' defence, rather than resorting to a complementary
one. This may be in this instance because the troublesome unconscious
fantasy was about belonging.

In this discussion we started to pick up the difficulty from the case
material. Temporarily I forgot how Mr Knights had presented his
immediate problem. But in this illustration, as in the last one, the
supervisor very clearly expressed a very strong feeling when he said,
"This is what I feel in relation to the student's work." It was his feeling
of "loading the poor girl" (par. 9) and being "unfair" to her which can
give us some indication of the strength of the feeling in the client. In
this particular case, I believe, the feelings were about belonging.*

This example does, I think, exemplify the point I made in Chapter
Two (page 35) that it is the detail and not the overall fact of the transference with which one has to work. It is not enough to know that Celia
may feel unlovable in relation to parent-figures. It is too global and
does not allow for the different meanings we all attribute to the word
"love". The important thing is what that word means to the client and
what particular feeling is getting re-enacted with the worker. The importance to Roderick of the older Celia and of the sixteen-year old Hazel
only starts to have some meaning in terms of his particular confusion
about an older sister who might have been his mother, and the fact that
when he was Hazel's age his most prominent adoptive parent started
to fade away. It is interesting that no one in the seminar asked why he
had not, as an adult, found out the truth about his mother. Perhaps to
him it was too dangerous to know, until he had had some help with
his feelings about this.

POSTSCRIPT
"Elizabeth's deep feeling of respect for the client's privacy was important. She was on principle reluctant to 'dig too deep'. But as the

---

* Infantile feelings of need and then of anger at that need not being met are often
very intense. The anger is felt to be destructive. If the need is not met within rea-
sonable time, if the feeling is not mitigated by constant proof that the provider or
another is not damaged, or if the fantasy is confirmed in reality, the feeling often
persists into adulthood either consciously or unconsciously and gets transferred on
to other people. Celia had her worst fears confirmed when she could see her attention-
getting sister was damaged. She probably reasoned with the omnipotent, magical
thinking of young children that she had done that. Roderick's more prominent
parent, his father, died. This may have felt like retribution to Roderick after the
years he had wanted to get closer to his shadowy mother or sister, if only he could
find out to whom he really belonged. No wonder feelings about belonging were
dangerous to this couple in connection both with the unsatisfied need and their
fear of what might happen if they dared to try to get closer—a burden to carry around
and one constituting a big psychological problem for them internally and in their
relationship with one another.

placement continued, she was able to move from her earlier entrenched position, and for me this was one of the most interesting things on the placement.

"Last January (a year later) I was able to apply for the discharge of Roderick's order, four months before natural termination. I wondered whether I was colluding with their flight from the problem, but I think I had achieved as much as I could and I didn't want it to run into something meaningless. Roderick thought that the most useful work was done in the first six months. He said, 'Probation is the best thing that happened to me,' but he was able to talk about the conflict he felt about it as a punishment and as a helping process.

"I was never again able to involve Celia to the extent that I would have liked. But there was a continued change of an appreciable kind in Roderick. He arrived at a position where he no longer regarded Celia as all 'hard', and was more able to recognise her feminine qualities. And this enabled him to change his own response to her. And he eventually got himself into a regular job which was much more in line with his abilities (i.e. skilled, as opposed to unskilled). One of my male colleagues took over Hazel's supervision. Ideally I would have chosen a woman, but when I discussed it with Hazel, she opted for a man, and we were short of women staff at the time. My colleague had difficulty in getting her co-operation, but she has been holding a regular job and is much more part of the family.

"From the grape-vine I have learned that the family continues to function as a unit, but are still aligning themselves with people who are currently known to us, and are thus still one step removed."

Summary

The Supervisor's Reflection.

Mr Knights, another experienced probation officer, expressed his supervisory problems in terms of his concern that he was being "unfair" to his student, Miss Regan, and that "I have loaded the poor girl too much with very important things that are going on in this case."

This appeared to be a very strong reflection of the burdensome defence and unconscious and mixed feelings about unfairness shared by a husband and wife, both of whom had great doubts about whether or not they really belonged in their families of origin, and suspicion that needing to belong, wanting to belong and then trying to belong could only cause pain and destruction. The husband, Roderick, had been an adopted child, with one elderly adoptive parent much more predominant than the other, and he had never known whether or not his much older sister was really his natural mother. The wife, Celia, had never known her father and had been brought up in a rigid, Victorian atmosphere with her mother and step-father, having to compete for attention with a much younger, mentally handicapped half-sister.

These mixed feelings and the defence against them had been carried over into the marriage and expressed, after Roderick had had a casual affair, and Celia had "paid him back" with an even more casual one, by continued guilt, depression and discomfort in both of them two years later.

Roderick was placed on probation for an offence committed several months after his adultery. Mr Knights had tried to focus his work on the marital relationship, but Celia who had had a long association with the department in another connection, increasingly became more elusive. Roderick probably played into this and unconsciously wanted to keep her out of the work and not share his bit of belonging to an officer. When things materially improved, Celia started shoplifting. After she had been fined by a Court, she imported into the household Hazel, her sixteen-year-old daughter of her first marriage. Soon Hazel shoplifted and was placed on a supervision order. Miss Regan became her officer and made good initial contact with her and with Celia, who then committed another offence.

At the time the case was first presented to the group, Miss Regan was wondering whether to recommend the making of an order, and Mr Knights was *worrying about the burden he was placing on her.*

The Student's Reflection.

But the Court gave a suspended sentence to Celia, who, at first, was overtly very angry. Then Miss Regan lost her as a client, expressed great doubts as to whether she could interfere without the legal mandate, and was only half-hearted in her invitation to Celia to keep up the regular appointments. She was over-concerned with "justice", about which she argued with Mr Knights, believing that he was too theoretical and that casework was about warmth and humanity. But she lost Celia after the latter had cried and showed her distress in an interview. She found this difficult to handle and it sounded as if she had not been able to hold on to her own knowledge that casework is often about pain. Her own problem of whether she could remain involved was compounded by the client's projection of the unconscious fear of the pain that she would feel if she dared to belong, and then not to belong, when Miss Regan left.

The group started discussing Celia's problem in terms of her feeling so unlovable and of having lost three husbands. But this was too global to be useful, the word, "love", having such very different connotations for different people. But through some associative thinking about the histories of Roderick and Celia and the particular meaning of the adultery, it seemed that the transference problem of this couple with each other and with the workers was more about who belonged to whom. The strength of this anxiety was felt directly by the sensitive and experienced supervising officer. The defence against it, the need to keep away from it, was acted-out by the less experienced, less confident student.

Roderick used his period on probation fairly effectively, becoming stronger as a man and perceiving his wife as more feminine, thereby making some shift in his outward attitude to her, which would then have effected some change in her behaviour. But Celia continued to "flirt" with the Service and with other delinquents, as she had done for several years before her own offences, still too afraid to belong to an officer for a given period of time.

I think there was a very weighty transference operating in this case, and that the work would have got stuck at various points with any worker, unless the countertransference was felt and noted and some clarification made with the clients of the particular fears and doubts about belonging.

There was a strong adolescent flavour about this case expressed both in the extreme reactions of the clients and in the use they made of Hazel, whom they imported into the family when she was the age that Celia had been when she conceived her, and the age at which Roderick's adoptive father had started to fade out. The adolescence was reflected by the group's behaviour, which became temporarily extreme in tone, members exaggerating beyond the given facts. This lessened when one member put into words that she "felt stuck" in the adolescence of Roderick and Celia.

The Group's Reflection.

Example III

THE MANAGEMENT OF THE THUMPING

In the two previous examples the group's reflection of what was going on in the case was of limited duration, and the feelings underlying the acting-out were fairly soon brought into conscious knowledge and handled directly in words. In this example the group's reflection is more vivid and the acting-out more extreme.

In the first and third chapters of this monograph I stressed the difficulties of working with the reflection process and that we had not got very far. This example is one of a group's failure. In the first seminar the supervisor showed that on her own she had picked up the most important facet of the worker's reflection after the first few interviews. She had dealt with this appropriately in the supervision, although she had manifested the reflection herself in subtler terms. But in the two seminars recorded, the group acted-out and employed defences against other feelings in the case. In the second seminar the defence was acted-out even more strongly, as were the feelings when, temporarily, the defence could be dropped.

A colleague and I were joint leaders. I was one of the main actors, but she was able to retain her calm and indicate which was the troublesome area. But we were left feeling dissatisfied, carrying a foreign body (page 47). We were not able to translate this into words explicit enough to be of much help to the supervisor and her worker on a case which, at first, did not appear too difficult.

Again in this example, as in the first, the supervisor expressed concern about the autonomy of the worker, worrying that she had over-supervised when her supervision seemed most appropriate, and then later inappropriately overteaching. It may not be coincidence that this has come up so blatantly in two of the four examples, and I shall return to this point in the final chapter.

The summary is on page 114.

THE CASE OF MR AND MRS HARRIS
Presenting:	Marriage Guidance Council tutor:	Mrs Jean Elland
Worker:	Marriage Guidance Counsellor:	Mr Robin Jones
Family:	Husband:	Mr Harris, aged 26, miner
	Wife:	Mrs Harris, aged 23, housewife
	Children:	daughter, aged 3
		son, aged 1

Mrs Elland works in the Midlands and was the one M.G.C. tutor   1
in a London-based seminar which was open to supervisors in any

social work setting. She was often an influential member in taking the work of the group forward. The group met weekly for two years, during the first year working on their own cases, during the second on those of the officers they supervised.

Mrs Elland started her presentation. "Well, now a bit about my worker first. His name is Robin. He's twenty-nine and married. Previously, before coming to work for Marriage Guidance, he had done some youth service training as a voluntary youth leader. Roughly, he's done a year's work with us. Of course, in our agency the work is very much part-time. 2

"And Robin carries a caseload of about three and he does some occasional group sessions for us with young people. He attends a fortnightly group which I lead and he has individual supervision with me about every three months. I feel, by and large, that Robin is a very observant man and able to pick up a good deal of non-verbal communication. And he once said to me he likes being where the other person is when he's interviewing. 3

"Now I saw him yesterday. He knew, of course, that I was bringing this here today. I had discussed this with him previously and so I asked him what he felt would be appropriate for me to convey. He brought two cases to the session. One was a case going back to last April which he had just closed. He came out of it very well and we didn't spend much time on that, as he wanted to discuss this new case. I think it might be appropriate for me to read you his report. It is not long and might convey something. Here it is." 4

Mrs Elland read Mr Jones' summary of five interviews. The first interview was a joint one and it was followed by four singles, two with each partner. Mr Harris was a miner and literally on strike, but perhaps metaphorically so as well. He was twenty-six and described as "toothy-looking", and, because of his accent, difficult to understand. Mrs Harris, aged twenty-three, not very pretty, was articulate and did most of the speaking throughout the first interview. Her story was occasionally punctuated by Mr Harris who either denied or altered her version, but had little to say for himself. They had been married six years and had two small children. Mrs Harris had had a nervous breakdown when she was seventeen (apparently at the age at which she married) and their main problem at the moment, she said, was her mother who was also subject to "nerves". She could not be left on her own and Mrs. Harris was now spending an increasing amount of her time at her parents' home, often sleeping there. But that was not the only problem. There were other things such as Mr Harris' tantrums and his masturbation. Mrs Harris claimed that their inability to have sexual intercourse was due to this, and it was a great disappointment to her. Mr Harris was 5 embarrassed, and "it was agreed that they would have two further sessions separately."

A week later Mrs Harris came with the three-year-old daughter 6 who prohibited much discussion. Again Mrs Harris talked first about the problem she encountered with her mother. She felt she had to be responsible, to take the weight off her father's shoulders. Her mother, despite the attention she required, seemed a remote figure. It was to her father that Mrs Harris turned when she was in trouble. Mr Jones attempted to lead her to consider the effects on her husband, but this was of no avail. But she then turned the subject to sexual matters and said that she considered her husband to be abnormal. She was humiliated by his masturbation. Even when it did take place, sexual intercourse was unsatisfactory because it lasted so short a time. Mr Jones ended this part of the report with the question, "What can I do? Mrs Harris sounds so hopeless."

Later that day Mr Jones had an interview with a rather desperate 7 Mr Harris. He was lonely on his own, but was just coping. He gave pathetic glances at some books left behind by his daughter. He laid most of the blame on his mother-in-law and saw no prospect of any improvement; he even contemplated the day when he would live with them. His job would not allow him to move. "If only we could be on our own," he kept repeating. And yet he continually indicated that there was something more, but he could not say what it was. The solution, he thought, was only just round the corner and could be reached fairly easily.

The next week there were two more interviews. Mrs Harris reported 8 that the situation had not changed. She was still at her parents' home. For the first time she could talk more logically about her husband. She felt frightened by him and could not cope with his moods and tantrums. Again she talked of her humiliation sexually—never had she felt truly a woman with her husband. Why had she not left before? She felt the pull of her parent's home and this was new. Her feelings towards her husband seemed to be those of fear mixed with contempt. Mr Jones asked if she loved him. "I just don't know," she sighed. The future frightened her too. She felt that as the children grew up she would be drawn nearer to her husband. "The future seems so black," she said.

At the beginning of his interview Mr Harris could not see any prob- 9 lem except that of his mother-in-law. Everything would be fine if only his wife would come home. Mr Jones tried to get him to talk about his temper. Very reluctantly he admitted that he was easily aroused, but claimed that his wife was so difficult to live with; she must take the blame. Mr Harris found it difficult to consider his own feelings, but later asked, "Am I crazy? What about a psychiatrist?" Mr Jones had thought of this previously and there and then made an appointment with Dr. C. His report continued, "When I had done this, Mr Harris blurted out that it was all too much; he was quite happy talking to me. He went on to talk of being confused; he just couldn't sort out how he felt. For the first time he admitted that things were much more serious than he cared to believe. I felt a great pity for him. He seemed such a little boy looking for a non-existent mother."

My colleague asked if there were any questions before Mrs Elland 10 went on to tell us about the supervisory session with Mr Jones. There were questions about the referral and allocation. For some time the group seemed more interested in how the M.G.C. worked than in the case material. But it was established that Mrs Harris also came from a mining family, that she was an only child, and that one of her reasons for getting married was to get out of her parents' home "which was a bit small". There was no more available information about Mr Harris.

Mrs Elland described the session she had had with Mr Jones the 11 previous day. "First I asked him to tell me more about the joint inter-view—how they had affected each other and how they behaved towards each other and to him. And usually Robin is very good at this—good at observing and picking up the type of communication. But he found it very difficult in the interview—something he normally doesn't find hard at all he found quite difficult. He couldn't say what had gone on between them. He said the wife took all the initiative. She was the leader, as it were. But it wasn't exactly controlling. He couldn't see it as being a controlling factor. He saw her as mostly unconcerned. She was anxious to talk—to Robin—but she was unconcerned about her husband, but not really trying to dominate him. In fact, she ignored him. And she brought out the bit about masturbating and so on in a rather ignoring way, not turning to him in any way at all."

"She brought it up jolly quickly, didn't she?" 12

"A punishing thing to do with a stranger there." 13

"Yes. Robin said the husband was quite embarrassed and uncom- 14 municative, just punctuating with his remarks and not really getting himself across. And Robin felt that sharing was a difficulty for both of them. She obviously couldn't share with him and displayed this in the interview. And he couldn't really share her parents. They kept on intruding in one way or another.

"And then I left that for the moment and asked him what he felt 15 the single interviews had achieved, because it had been his idea to split them, and I asked him why this was so important at this point. And he said that it was this non-communication on the part of the husband—that he just felt he couldn't get through to him. And then he said he didn't push him, but felt pushed into seeing them separately, because he couldn't think how he could deal with it otherwise. He felt he couldn't get at the sharing and the communication without seeing them separately. I don't know whether it is so, but I felt he was very much pushed by them into splitting them."

"What did they feel about being seen individually?"

"The wife was agreeable, and the husband just went along with it, as he does everything apparently. But I am not sure how appropriate it was for Robin to split them at that point—whether it would have been helpful from the clients' point of view for him to have continued jointly for a bit longer. What I did say to him was that I was a bit afraid that in single interviews he was beginning to lose the marriage —that he was seeing these two as individuals and that he wasn't linking the individual work back into the marital situation. We spent the rest of the supervisory session on looking at this aspect. He said that in the singles the wife had been free to pursue her own ideas. He let her talk and built up a relationship with her. I went along with this. He said the husband's interview had been mainly concerned with his anxieties over his mental state and his sexual inadequacy. And I felt Robin had colluded with this. I tried to convey to him that he had been presented with the marriage, because this half-separated couple had come along together. I thought it would be a pity if he lost this and didn't link what he was doing in the individual sessions back into the marriage again."

In the first part of the discussion a few useful points were raised about the case, and a half-hearted attempt was made to look at the interaction. The situation of rivalry that Mr Harris was in with his wife's father was mentioned. "What does she turn to her father for?"

"She says if she were in trouble, if there were any difficulties over money, if there was any problem, she would turn to father first."

"But she was unable to look at what this might do to her husband."

"And his being on strike would obviously make this situation worse."

The group thought it was fairly usual in a mining community for a daughter to remain parent-orientated. "In mining communities the man moves into the wife's family rather than the other way round, doesn't he? I wonder if he has been accepted by her parents."

"Yes," said Mrs. Elland, "when you mentioned a little while ago whether Mr Harris could assert himself and get his rights, it didn't feel like that when Robin was discussing them, but more like a situation handled by encompassing the people whom the children marry, rather than by setting up another unit. So it felt like as if her family couldn't be shared with him."

"You mean that he hasn't been allowed to opt into her family. But, particularly as she was an only child, she might find it very difficult to share."

"Yes, it feels more about moving in than moving out."

"So, perhaps it is not so surprising that Robin found it difficult in the interview to get the husband in," I said. "Probably Mr Harris couldn't let himself in and she couldn't let him come in. You said she seemed to ignore him."

"In this case Robin seemed to be saying he can't be where they are in 27 a joint interview. He can't handle it. It's almost as if he's saying he can't be in two places at once. He can't be with the marriage. He's with two separate people."

"This may be very important diagnostically," I said. "Can he work 28 with other couples in threesomes?"

Mrs Elland thought that he could do this and that he had felt pushed 29 into separating these two, and then had got confused about where he was working. "And when we discussed it, he could see that these two people didn't seem to bear much relation to each other. He interviewed her and he interviewed him, and there could have been two separate cases."

"When he saw you was he worried at having got them separately?" 30

"He was beginning to. He wasn't at first. The first single interviews 31 he thought were all right, but by the end of the second interviews things were getting so divergent."

"It's interesting that the child left some books behind and the father 32 saw these . . . and gave them pathetic glances."

"Did he take them home with him?" 33

"A small attempt to connect up, despite the single interviews." 34

"I don't follow. Can you explain?" 35

"Unconsciously, perhaps, it was important to the wife that the 36 books were left behind for him to see, so that he knew she had been there. There are often unconscious reasons for forgetting things."[4]

The group expressed its unease in the further separation of referring 37 the husband off to a psychiatrist. The anxiety of the husband as to whether he was mad seemed to have got into Mr Jones. Or was this just Mr Jones' inexperience? According to his report, immediately after the referral was arranged, Mr Harris had said it all felt too much; he was quite happy talking to Mr Jones. What was all too much?

Mrs Elland explained that there was a very close liaison with Dr C. 38 who led a supervision group in which Mr Jones had been a member.

But it seemed too much or too little for the group. They became 39 fractious, started fidgeting and complained about a "smokescreen". To escape from the frustration they started making irrelevant suppositions beyond the material in the single interviews. For all this Mrs Elland ticked them off smartly, "We haven't got as far as that yet." She had not had time to discuss the single interviews with Mr Jones. For about the fifth time she said, "I was concerned about what was going on in the joint interview, and how he was being pushed away from the marriage. This was what we spent the time on."

"We can't get into the interaction of this case," said my colleague, 40 "but perhaps this is because it all feels so uninteractive."

"I think we're getting ahead of ourselves," said Mrs Elland. "I was   41
still at the stage of the joint interview and his splitting them up."

"Yes," persisted my colleague, "but what did you and what did he   42
think about the interaction of this couple?"

"I felt he hadn't really been aware of this until I actually asked him   43
about it, or made him think about it. It wasn't until I questioned him
that he pulled it out how separate they were. And then he began to
question what he was doing in the singles, but we hadn't got as far as
linking the two."

COMMENT

". . . how separate they were. And then he began to question what he
was doing in the singles, *but we hadn't got as far as linking the two.*" This,
perhaps, is the most important statement of Mrs Elland's presentation.

In coming together Mr and Mrs Harris expressed a hope that they
might be able to do something about a problem of being very separate
in their marriage. In the joint interview with Mr Jones they showed
how very difficult it was for them to relate together. Mrs Harris virtually
ignored Mr Harris and was "unconcerned" about him (par. 11). But
their underlying anxiety about what would happen if they came closer
together communicated itself to Mr Jones to such an extent that he felt
"pushed" (pars. 15 and 39) into going along with their defence of retreating from the difficulty (which they had expressed in various ways;
physically, by her moving back to her parents' home and by their
inability to have intercourse; and mentally, by Mrs Harris' refusal to
take any notice of her husband). Mr Jones joined in the defence and
separated them out into single interviews.

Although Mr. Jones was normally able to pick up a good deal of
non-verbal communication between people, he could not with this
couple relate to the degree of separation they portrayed when together.
He could not get it into his report. But with the help of his supervisor
he could describe very vividly what they made him feel like; he could
not be "in two places at once" (par. 27). They and he lost the hope,
and then, of course, he got even more despair in the single interviews.
"What can I do?" he asked. "Mrs Harris sounded so hopeless."

Mrs Elland did not act-out and did not join in this part of the
reflection process. She did a good piece of supervision, noticed that
the marriage was getting even more lost in the single interviews, expressed her concern, and drew her worker's attention to what was
happening. He had walked into the trap that was set for him. Her
alerting him about this proved extremely fruitful, as the reader will
hear in the next session. His action was not disastrous, and when Mr
and Mrs Harris again expressed the hope, he *heard* the signal and
reacted to it (pars. 46 and 47 ahead). He and the clients were able to

get out of this part of the fix and it is this ,"alongside the more practised understanding of the anguish . . . that really affects the course of any helping process" (page 42).

But what was the irritation (par. 39) about in this group? It may have been partly to do with the members' envy of Mrs Elland. In as far as she had taken the supervision, she had done well. She did not present the group with a problem; she robbed them of an obvious task. It is always easier for a group to work if there is a definition of the problem.

But obviously there were other problems ahead. The group was very much concerned about what felt like a premature referral to Dr. C. In Mr Harris' own words, "it felt too much". But Mrs Elland resisted any attempt to take the discussion further forward (pars. 39 and 41). Perhaps she was also reflecting the separation in the way that she got stuck on this in the supervision, unable to link the two important factors—the separation in the single interviews and the non-interaction in the joint. But it was a much subtler manifestation than that of Mr Jones.

And the degree of separation got into the group. As Mrs Elland resisted any attempts to take the discussion further, and as the other members became more fractious and more speculative about the material, complaining bitterly that they had not got enough facts (when there were plenty), the gulf widened between her and them.

With Mrs Elland we were stuck on the separation and, with her, acted it out. We expressed despair and were unable to look in any detail at the fears and feelings that might have been behind this to which there were clues in the material.

A FORTNIGHT LATER

"Shall I go straight on . . . ?"   44

"Does anyone want a recap? . . . No."   45

"Well, I had a supervisory session yesterday and we began by looking   46
at how Robin had used the last one and what had happened in the interim. And he said that he had become aware of two things. One was the awareness of the non-marriage, the fact that I had brought up my fears about losing the sharing bit in the marriage. And secondly, the other thing he felt had particularly come out was the family and the social setting, and so he'd thought about taking up these points in the next interview. What actually happened the next week was that the wife missed her appointment. She 'phoned the secretary to say that one of the children had measles and she sounded very upset on the 'phone. And the secretary took this at its face value and felt this was genuine. And Mrs Harris asked if she could book an appointment for the next week and would like to come on such and such a day and, when the secretary checked, this was the day that the husband was coming. Fortunately Robin spotted this and it registered with him and he felt this a very

fortuitous happening. He decided that this was a good opportunity to have them both coming at the same time.

"And she took up this offer and in point of fact, although she's still not 47 living at home, they actually came together, which was different from the first joint interview when they came from different parts of the town."

Again Mrs Elland read Mr Jones' notes of his interview, but pre- 48 ceded the account by saying, "I was a bit disappointed, I suppose, because the notes weren't as full as I'd hoped. He was writing the notes for himself, but on this occasion I also wanted him to write them for me. And this he found very difficult and there was a lot missing, and I wondered what this was about really."

Mr and Mrs Harris had come together. Mr Harris had talked about 49 his visit to Dr. C. He felt he had been helped by the expert who had asked a lot of questions. He had accepted her explanation that the masturbation was "like a baby's comforter". He was now able to talk about his masturbation. He'd always done it. He had had a difficult home life and had never been happy. They hadn't had normal inter-course for two years. Mr Jones had felt a great deal of sympathy for "this poor dejected boy". But his wife was coming home the next Saturday. Why Saturday? It was then Monday, and there was a lot of stuff to move.

Mrs Harris talked about her mother, who demanded so much 50 attention that Mrs Harris could not let her down. Mrs Harris showed great ambivalence to both Mr Harris and her mother, but would not admit this.

Mr and Mrs Harris now felt they could cope with each other, and 51 contraception seemed the uppermost thing in their minds. In talking together some tension seemed to have been released. They were both more willing to be honest with each other about how they felt. The interview ended with an arrangement for them to visit the F.P.A. to be followed by another interview with Mr. Jones in a fortnight's time.

Before Mrs Elland went on to talk about the supervision, there were 52 a few comments about the report. Mrs Elland again mentioned her disappointment that the report left out Mr Jones' part in the interview, and that, when she had particularly asked him to write something fuller for her, he had not been able to do so.

"Perhaps he feels like the couple being given expert advice. What 53 does he feel about his work being discussed here?"

"In a way he seemed gratified that I'd decided to use his work, and 54 he thanked me very much yesterday for giving him the opportunity. But I certainly feel it's had quite an effect on him. Because something I was talking about in the individual supervision he fed into the group discussion which followed when we were looking at somebody else's case. So I think he was really trying to use the material."

"Is he really as uninvolved as he sounded in that report?" 55

"No, he's not uninvolved with clients. What were you thinking?" 56

"It just came over to me as a very uninvolved kind of interview with 57
two people who were desperately unhappy."

"I don't think this is so, because he's very sensitive. I wonder, though, 58
if he were not wanting to present himself as being involved—as if he
thought it wasn't the right thing to be."

"Perhaps it's a bit daunting having your work exposed to a group of 59
people you don't know."

Mrs Elland described the supervision. "Well, the first thing I took 60
up with him was this bit of their coming together. And then I asked
about Mr Harris' visit to Dr C., who had come across as the expert.
She is a woman, yes. And Robin thought it was helpful that Dr. C. had
not taken it up in terms of the marriage—helpful from his point of
view, because it determined their roles. Dr. C. had felt her task had
been to help Mr Harris with his mental disturbance and that it was
Robin's role to help with the marriage, and this has been definitely
understood between them. And Robin also thought this was helpful
from the client's point of view, because Mr Harris had got a good deal
of reassurance from her about his difficulty and now began to talk to
Robin quite a lot about it, and about how he felt. There's no further
appointment with Dr. C. So I came away feeling that this probably
had been a useful thing to have happened, even though it could have
gone the other way. I think, maybe, that it's got something to do with
the relationship between our office and this particular psychotherapist
that made it work out all right."

"What did Robin feel about it?" 61

"He was quite pleased because he felt that Mr Harris had gained 62
from the reassurance that he wasn't mad, that he wasn't crazy."

"Did he feel that this was something that could only be given by 63
someone else?"

"Yes, I think so. Or he thought that this was much more reassuring 64
coming from the expert, and he mentioned the word expert on one or
two occasions. Much more reassuring coming from the expert, because
Robin was working with them on other things, not on madness or
craziness or anything like that. But, I think, as it happened, it worked
out all right.

"I found out quite a bit more about the husband's background. The 65
father was a miner and he was a 'thumper'. I don't know whether you
know what thumping miners are, but they're a rumbustical sort of
. . . not viciously violent . . . but they do go round thumping people.
But all his family—father, mother and sister—looked down on Mr
Harris as being strange, quiet, always alone and a bit of a clown. And I
got a picture of Mr Harris with his peculiar toothy appearance, quiet

and not a thumper like his father, and looked down upon by his family for being so strange. His mother was a controlling woman and her husband had to thump her when he couldn't stand it any longer. He sounded a quiet man, but more assertive than Mr Harris. Only when it gets too much he thumps. His arms go waving and he throws things. But Mr Harris can't do this.

"The wife seemed to present herself in this interview as a martyr,   66
and at this point I asked Robin to explain to me much more what he meant by this and what he thought the interaction was about. And he went on at some length to describe what the two were like together, but *he couldn't write this* down on paper. And he said that when they first came together they were talking about separation, it was all about separation. But this time they were talking about each other and how they might get together. And he said that the husband was strange and quiet, but much more relaxed, and his wife very much a martyr, feeling that she'd been put on and rather enjoying being put on."

"A martyr to whom?"   67

"She likes to feel that her mother needs her. It's to her mother, not   68
her husband, that she's a martyr."

"Difficult to be a martyr to a strange, quiet husband."   69

"But she is now a martyr to Dr. C. Obviously something quite   70
important happened for Mr. Harris with Dr. C."

"Did she have the wind taken out of her sails by the reassurance he   71
got?"

"Losing her alibi."   72

The group could not let Mrs Elland finish her presentation and she   73
seemed to feel these interruptions as untimely punctuations. On this occasion and on several others she proceeded with her account. "And then came the bit about the contraception. And I took this up with Robin, because I didn't think he would just introduce it willy-nilly. I wondered what their actual difficulty was. And he said he saw the F.P.A. in this instance rather like Dr. C. The F.P.A. would discuss methods of contraception with them and it would be his job to discuss the feelings about contraception."

"Seems to be a big split between the mechanics of something and   74
the feelings about it."

"Did Robin introduce the F.P.A.?"   75

"Yes. He said, 'If you want some expert advice on this, the people   76
to go to is the F.P.A.' "

"He's very much got his own style, hasn't he?"   77

"Dealing with his insecurity."   78

"Is it just his own insecurity?" I said. "There's splitting all over the   79
place in this case, as well as in his behaviour. Is this his usual style, or is it just on this case he seems to become the manager? I was fascinated

by your description of the tight division of labour between him and the psychotherapist. It was so well worked out. Clients aren't usually as tidy as this. But Mr Harris got tidy reassurance."

"He used to be in her group before he moved into mine. I think this division of labour is understood between them." 80

"I don't get this martyr business really." (Note the same juxtaposition as before (pars. 66-72). The group seem to connect Mr Harris' visit to Dr. C. and Mrs Harris' being a martyr). 81

Again Mrs Elland cut across the discussion ."Robin didn't feel at all certain that she would return on Saturday. And the other bit that I put to him was this concept, which he found quite difficult, about the husband carrying the badness and the wife's projection of this, linking with her own fears about her previous illness and that of her mother. And we went over this once or twice, because I think this is a difficult concept for new workers to get hold of. And he did get this, but he wrote it down. And I'm quite sure that he's going to tackle this in the wrong way. I could understand him using this with some couples, but with a couple like this who seem very immature and not very articulate, I don't know what he'll do with it. 82

"Well, that was about it, but I got the feeling that *he was expecting me to do the work* and take up what I wanted; not the other way round. Oh, but another thing I queried was whether he should go on in joint interviews. Or whether he still felt that there were things that he ought to take up in individual interviews with this couple. It seemed to me as if, because of what I had said or done in the previous session, he had deliberately changed course. I was almost saying, 'You've almost done this because of what I've said. Is this really right? You know, it's your client.' But he said it felt right to have taken it back into joints. But now he's done it, I don't know whether I ought to have suggested some combination might be more appropriate." 83

"That's a funny thing to say." I said. "The clients 'accidentally-on-purpose' fixed their interviews on the same day and, when offered one at the same time, chose to come together. Because of what you had previously said, Robin was able to pick this up—to notice it and arrange the appointment accordingly. Why do you want to go back on something obviously very effective?" 84

"Because they're his clients. He thought there were things that needed to be said in individual interviews. I don't know how much was the clients or him." 85

"But in the second joint interview the husband could discuss his masturbation in the presence of, if not with, his wife. She cancelled her single for a very good reason—the measles—but she asked for another on the same day as her husband was coming and accepted one at his time. Perhaps she knew where the work needed to be at that moment. 86

Robin picked up the signal, but she sent it out. And now you're frightened that your work helped him to pick up the clients' signal." I was getting rather cross.

"Yes, it's a highly familiar thing to me as a supervisor. One's torn   87
between one's convictions and not wanting to take over the case from the worker. I know Robin gets critical when he's pushed, and he sometimes pushes me into being critical. Is he pushing me into controlling the situation?"

"All right. All right," I said, leaning forward, throwing out an arm   88
and getting even crosser. "The case is full of controlling or expert women—mothers who control through their nerves and probably could do with a thump, a wife who isn't thumped enough, a psychotherapist who thumps most effectively . . ." I was doing a good piece of thumping myself.

"It's as though," said my very much calmer colleague, "this is the   89
main interaction that's getting passed around." I withdrew into my chair, frowning heavily and very cross with Mrs Elland.

"Oh, dear," said someone. "I find this very difficult in terms of the   90
supervision I do myself."

The group took flight and started to discuss whether group or in-   91
dividual supervision was more effective.

"Red herring. Red herring."   92

"Sorry."   93

But there were more red herrings. We went miles and miles from the   94
work in hand. The squabble again got into the whole group. "Can I ask about the husband?" said a plaintive voice. The question was not clear and Mrs Elland replied in terms of the worker. The group moved off once more. It was learnt that Mr Jones would be leaving and moving to another area. The group said it felt cheated. But Mrs Elland had made it clear that he would be available to work with this and his other cases for another two months.

"May I ask about the husband?" said the same plaintive voice again.   95
"Last time you answered about the worker."

But the question was evaded again. "It's like a smokescreen," said   96
one member. (The same word had been used in the discussion a fortnight previously.)

"The wife virtually asked for a joint interview and yet somehow I   97
never actually get hold of what happened."

"As a group it seems like trying to catch a fish in the water with your   98
bare hands. You've got it for a second, then it's gone. Flash."

"I don't know whether this is relevant," I said hesitantly, "but, if   99
it is so difficult to catch the fish, perhaps one has to resort to management, or that's what it feels like. Only expert management has results. Robin seems to be managing the case and parcelling it out. And then

you get frightened that you over-manage your worker. Is this a facet of the case that gets acted-out—a facet strong enough to get through to you on the second supervision and you start worrying about your management? And it so gets through to us that we go off into the most incredible flights as to how you manage your workers when they are leaving. Is this something to do with the case or with the setting? Is Robin a manager in all his cases, splitting them off into bits? In a way I had almost hoped last time that he would learn that it doesn't necessarily help to use the specialist and that the fantasied madness was better held within the one piece of work. But, in actual fact, it did help the husband. Temporarily—whether permanently, we don't know— it was very effective. But what I don't understand is that you get worried by what seemed a good bit of supervision; you picked up the splitting that was going on, so that Robin was able to pick up the wife's attempt to get them together again—a more belligerent signal than just leaving the child's books behind. But in the second supervision it sounds as if you over-taught him—over-managed the teaching. You said it felt such a difficult concept to understand. And it is, particularlv when it is not clear in the material. And we're not clear about it here. We know Mrs Harris had some form of breakdown and her mother has nerves and that he was scared he might be mad. But we don't really know what the *actual* feelings are that might be projected. We know that something about being a martyr is going on in the transference—not much more. Robin must have felt over-taught if he had to take notes on it and trot it out at the next session—a too wholesale and undigested take-over. Is this the case or is it you and Robin?

"Well, I haven't had this bit about repeated referrals to other 100 agencies in his work. I can't remember another case where he has sent them off all the time."

"What about his feelings about expert advice? Experts? Has that 101 come in a lot of his other work?

"No, I don't think so." 102

"Is it the couple who are wanting experts? Are they underneath very 103 dependent?"

"Could it be to do with this group?" asked Mrs Elland. "He is very 104 keen to be professional."

"Yes, it may be to do with us and what we were talking about the 105 other week and the worker's fantasy about this group. But we're not being very expert today, and I think it's in the case as well. Both the clients are very despairing, according to how they were behaving and how we are still behaving in this group, and probably they're very dependent and very frustrated."

"We've had a few suggestions that this could be a daunting case. Is 106 this what we're denying in the group?" asked my colleague. "There is a frustrated and frustrating husband, who has never been able to thump, when thumping is part of the culture."

"Is it despair in this couple that they can't get the thumping into the marriage?" 107

"I would have thought it rather daunting to have been told that your masturbation was like a baby's comforter." 108

"It's difficult to imagine how one would feel about that." 109

"But that is what he *heard* and he didn't find it daunting. It seemed to release something. Afterwards he could talk about the difficulties of having intercourse. Some very important things are happening. They managed to get themselves a joint interview and they are thinking of moving back together again. But what I do query," I continued, "is whether the movement depends on management and experts. Because then, what happens when the expert leaves and stops managing? Are this couple very dependent?" 110

"I think Robin would deny that he is managing this case. He doesn't look on himself as a manager." 111

"It's time to stop, but I wish we could have got at this martyr business a bit more. Is Robin feeling a martyr to this group? And Mr Harris was the martyr in his first single—he was lonely but coping. We haven't got very far." 112

COMMENT

I do not think my comments about the management of this case were particularly helpful, other than in highlighting the type of defence that was being used by the worker, by the supervisor in the second supervisory session and by the group that so often took flight into enquiring how the M.G.C. managed its organisation. Management is obviously a very commonly used defence in social work. When it is difficult to understand what is happening in a situation within a family or between the clients and the worker, which is often the case, the easiest way of dealing with this anxiety of being so helpless and of not understanding, but also with any uncomfortable feelings that the clients may be projecting, is to *do* something, or to organise. At times this is appropriate; the clients may need a container or they may need someone temporarily to take responsibility for them and their arrangements. But sometimes it sets the work back and reinforces the client's defences when they are, in fact, asking for help in handling the problem in another way and to be given strength to let go of the habitual way of behaviour.

And Mr and Mrs Harris seemed to be asking for a change, although in the first joint interview their fear of what this change might mean overshadowed the initial request. They presented their problem of finding it difficult to get closer very clearly. They acted it out in the interview; Mrs Harris ignored her husband and he could only punctuate. To Mr Jones they felt as if they were in different places. His inability to continue to work in the joint interview, when he was capable of handling this situation with other couples, is indicative of the strength of their fear of how much they, like the porcupines, might prick, or, in this case, we might say, "thump", if they came closer and had more intercourse, both verbal and physical. He went along with the fear and ignored the hope and was thus left with the despair. But with some timely help from his supervisor he was able to get himself and the couple out of this immediate difficulty and then may have reinforced their hope of wanting to get together again on the following Saturday. It is not clear from his report or from what he said in the supervision whether he really held on to this. He said they were more interactive, but the material suggests that they were more interactive with him in each other's presence, but not very much with each other (pars. 49, 50, 60 and 86). They were both still speaking of their individual problems—Mr Harris about his masturbation, Mrs Harris about her mother. Mr Harris had briefly acquired an "alibi", a supportive woman figure who recognised where he was developmentally and who recognised his infantile needs. Mrs Harris had lost out and, no doubt, in the actual threesome interview recognised that her husband evoked more sympathy from Mr Jones. Not surprisingly he was unable to get the detail of the interaction into his report (par. 66), but in the supervision he was able to put into words that Mrs Harris came across very much as a martyr and rather enjoyed it. This was probably an important piece of detail of her habitual behaviour and was re-enacted with Mr Jones in relation to his closer (?) relationship with her husband who had been favoured by an interview with a specialist. She had lost out. And although Mr Jones said that in his single interviews with her he had been able to build up a relationship, it sounded to me as if he had, in fact, made more useful contact with Mr Harris. The latter had moved further by the second joint interview than his wife, but he had had additional attention.

For a couple wanting to resume intercourse, a visit to the F.P.A. is obviously most appropriate. And, as Mr Jones had previously referred Mr Harris to the specialist, it was appropriate in the total acting-out of the three of them that Mrs Harris should also have her referral and her bit of specialist attention. Where Mr Jones echoed the fear of this couple and emphasised their dependency was in his continued voicing, or echoing, of the "expert"*, leaving the most likely fantasy that only

---

* Mr Donald Ebert, a Canadian social worker, holding a Fellowship in the I.M.S., 1971-72, discovered, by accident, as it were, when doing a study on our intake procedure, that in his small sample any new client who mentioned the word "expert" opted out of treatment very quickly and we were unable to hold them. It would be useful to test the hypothesis that reliance on the "expert" is a bad prognostic factor for outcome.

"severe cases need experts" still hanging in the air.

The group may have been right and a pressure may have been going back to Mr Jones through Mrs Elland that this group were experts which put him on the defensive. But I think it is much more than that, and that the pressure came from the other side—that of the clients—as well, and was indicative of their own dependency needs which they could not express between themselves. Mrs Harris could express it in relation to her own parents and perhaps as she had had a breakdown during the year she got married, she had had difficulty then in freeing herself from close parental ties. Mr Harris could express it physically —"he seemed such a little boy looking for a non-existent mother".

It is easy being wise after the event. I can see now from the transcript that the dependency got into the supervision. Mr Jones and Mrs Elland acted-out a facet of the clients' behaviour—a request for dependency and a fear of meeting it by the other (par. 83). Mrs Elland was surprised that Mr Jones expected her to do the work. She tried very hard not to recognise the effectiveness of her earlier work, wanted "to change course", and was almost saying, "You've done this because of what I've said." In pars. 85 and 87 she continued to express her resistance against any dependency in her argument with me, and I got crosser and crosser.

Gross unmet dependency needs are usually coupled with a considerable amount of anger. This is the emotion the group expressed in both seminars when the management defence temporarily lifted. I was crosser in that second seminar than I remember being in a teaching situation for a long time (although my expressing it so forcibly would also be an indication of the professional strength of Mrs Elland; working groups of this type usually pick up which are the members with whom one can have a straight confrontation and with whom one can afford to express the emotion rather than the defence against that emotion).

That we expressed as much of the defence against the feelings as the worker did, is indicative, I think, of how difficult this case really was. In the initial presentation it seemed much less complicated, and certainly much less flamboyant, than those cases described in examples I and II. My colleague voiced the difficulty when she said, "This could be a daunting case." It is not always the most spectacular cases that are the most difficult. In fact the spectacle and the excitement derived from them are usually associated with the acting-out. And acting-out is a great tension reliever. The acting-out of this couple was much more muted, but probably much less tension relieving. They were left with much feeling, but a lot of it was too angry and painful to know about in more detail. The defence against this truly got into the worker, the supervisor and the group. I think Mrs Elland underestimated what her worker had got on his hands, if the couple could let him get into this area of the work. At this stage the reflection felt like a foreign body.

This was spoken to at the end of the discussion—whether a worker in this situation should attempt to get into the underlying problem, or whether management of the problem was a more appropriate way of dealing with it. Perhaps Mrs Elland unconsciously picked up something of the basic problem when she queried whether, after all, Mr Jones should be doing some of the work in single interviews. It is a big question whether work with strong, unmet dependency needs can be done in joint interviews. Can the joint interview get the couple to recognise and to meet within the relationship their own and the other's needs, without there being some prior experience of a tight one-to-one relationship in which some safer testing-out can be done first? I am not attempting to answer this important question in general terms here. But as regards this couple, they certainly needed the joint interviews at this point in the work to confirm the hope and to get them talking *with* each other. Only further material would show whether they needed to get into single work later on.

But we could not get at any of this in the seminar. We got a little further than the worker and the supervisor on her own, in that, at times, we expressed the feeling, and not just the defence. But we were unable to transfer this into understanding, or to put it into words that would help Mrs Elland in subsequent supervision. I would be interested to know more about the feeling of being cheated which the group expressed several times. What had this got to do with the case? Was Mrs Harris feeling very cheated that she had not had her father to herself?

There are many questions which were not even asked about the material which was presented, and the reader is left with these and, no doubt, with some of the frustrations that the group felt. (I have certainly re-experienced it as I have been writing, and it has taken me much longer than the two previous examples.) On this occasion the group was far from being "expert", which is not an uncommon phenomenon when a client is consciously or unconsciously asking for this. A fantasy that only expert help will do, or even will not do, allied as it usually is to idealisation and the subsequent despair, is enough to make most workers lose some of their usual expertise, particularly that part of it which is "never to be clever when clients ask you to be".

POSTSCRIPT
Mrs Harris did not return to her husband the following Saturday. And then the clients were lost. They failed to attend the next interview and did not respond to Mr Jones' friendly letter inviting them back. He assumed they remained separated.

Summary

Mrs Elland, an M.G.C. tutor, did not in the first seminar present a supervisory problem. The worker, Mr Jones, had strongly reflected the fear of his two clients, Mr and Mrs Harris, which underlay their hope that they might be less separate in their marriage. They expressed the hope initially by asking for a joint interview. But in this interview they expressed in action the fear of what might happen if they tried to realise this hope. Their ambivalence was typical of most people when asking for help. In the interview Mrs Harris ignored her husband and he could only punctuate her story.

The Worker's Reflection. Mr Jones was normally able to pick up non-verbal communications and note the process as well as the content of an interview, but with this couple he could not relate to the degree of separation they portrayed; as he said, he could not be "in two places at once". He separated them out into single interviews, but in the supervision he was able to see with his supervisor's help how he was losing the marriage and the hope, he and the couple being left with the despair.

Although Mrs Elland could help him with this, she still showed some reflection in that she was not able to link this piece of understanding of the non-interactive characteristic of the marriage with what had gone on in the single interviews.

Mr Jones had made what seemed to the group and to Mr Harris a premature referral for him to see a psychiatrist. Mrs Elland had thought this appropriate in terms of the way her team worked with this psychiatrist generally, and did not want to discuss it with the group. The members became fractious and despairing, unable, after a few half-hearted attempts to look at the interaction or lack of it, to take the discussion further forward. There arose an antagonism, or a split, between Mrs Elland and other members.

When Mrs Elland presented again a fortnight later, her previously reported supervision was proved to have been most effective. Mr Jones had recognised the client's renewed signal for a joint interview. In this interview they were more interactive, not with each other, but individually with Mr Jones in the presence of the other. The interview with the psychiatrist had proved helpful and reassuring to Mr Harris.

The Client's Transference. But Mrs Harris increasingly came across as a martyr to her mother, to her husband and to Mr Jones.

Mr Jones made another referral, this time to the F.P.A., appropriate in terms of a couple wanting to resume intercourse, and also in terms of his countertransference to the martyrdom, offering Mrs Harris some specialist attention to match that previously given to her husband.

The Group's Reflection. However in this seminar, the group became even more fractious than previously. The members interrupted Mrs

*The
Supervisor's
Reflection.*

*The Worker's
Reflection.*

*The Group's
Reflection.*

Elland's presentation of her supervision, and she obviously felt these interruptions as untimely punctuations. She would not allow them, and proceeded with her account, which she ended by expressing her doubts about the obvious effectiveness of her previous supervision. She wondered whether she had made her worker too dependent on her way of thinking, rejecting an appropriate dependency. Yet in the last supervision, she had inappropriately over-taught him. She had become the expert and he had taken down her words. She mentioned that he had tried to get her to do the work.

Unfortunately the group did not pick this up consciously, and at first only expressed the defence against the feeling usually coupled with unmet dependency needs—that of anger. It resorted to enormous flights from the case to how the M.G.C. managed its business, just as Mr Jones appeared to be managing the transference by organising referrals.

At one point I reflected the feeling which was being defended. I became extremely angry with Mrs Elland, verbally "thumping" her. (Mr Harris came from a thumping culture, but could not thump himself.) But we could not relate the feeling I expressed to the dependency needs either in the case, or as they were expressed in the work and in the supervision, reliance on the expert being grossly over-stressed in a variety of ways.

We ended the seminar talking only in terms of the defence— that of management, and one often used in social work. It left us feeling dissatisfied, the feeling, shied away from and not integrated into our thinking, remaining as an uncomfortable foreign body. We had not given the supervisor much help. And the clients were lost.

Example IV

A THREE-CORNERED AFFAIR

The three previous examples have illustrated not only different manifestations of the reflection process, but the additional problem of the
reflection of the case exaggerating normal difficulties in the teaching/
learning situation: the dependence or independence of the young
worker or student; the autonomy he should be allowed; how much he
should be taught or influenced; how much he should be left to find his
own way; how difficult a case he can be expected to handle.

This example is one where the major problem in the case reflected
the particular difficulties the supervisor was having in her department.

The case was presented in a London-based group during the period
of amalgamation of the social services. As local authority workers will
remember, it was a period of acute stress. At first there was anxiety
about one's own job for which one had to apply or about the decision
whether to take the opportunity of applying for promotion in the new
and much bigger hierarchical structure. There was competition with
colleagues. Then there were new teams, new seniors, new juniors and
new working companions. There was unease, suspicion and muddle, in
some instances fallen heads and disappointment, in others great insecurity from too rapid promotion. There were new welfare, mental
welfare and child care tasks to be learnt according to which of these
were not one's previous specialism.

One of the aims of this group for supervisors was to help them, not
necessarily to increase, but to hold on to, their existing casework and
supervisory skills during this period of colossal organisational change
in which the focus of their work had to widen radically.

The Summary is on page 124.

THE CASE OF MRS ANNIE SMITH
Presenting: Local Auth. Social
                Work Supervisor: Mrs Helen Mansfield
Worker: Local Auth. Social
                Worker: Mr John Taylor
Family: Mother: Mrs Annie Smith, aged 36
                Irregular co-habitee: Mr Nbongo, father of Caroline
                Children: Ben, aged 8; in care of another
                                   authority
                                   William, aged 14 months, illegiti-
                                   mate
                                   Caroline, aged 2 weeks, illegitimate

Mrs Mansfield presented this case a few months after the amalgamation   1
of the social services. Her previous experience had been in welfare, and
that of Mr Taylor had been in a children's department.

The new social service department was, like many others, very   2
short of staff, and over the previous few months there had been open
war between the basic-grade workers and the "establishment". It had
been a grim time for everyone over and above the re-organisational
difficulties. "It's difficult to explain," said the gentle Mrs Mansfield,
"just what an upsetting effect it has had, but you could literally feel it
tearing the team apart.

"And the anxiety and concern spilled over into the work situation,"   3
she continued. "Supervision sessions were taken up with feelings about
authority. I think every supervisor felt estranged from his or her team
at this period. It was a situation which I hadn't hoped to find myself
mixed up in—this political scene—and feeling that my team thought I
was outside it—regarded me as not having feelings, which, indeed, I had;
but I was more ambivalent, because I was in possession of information
which helped me to see it in a different light from the way they saw it.

"But to get on to John. It's a sort of three-cornered difficulty, really   4
—social worker, myself and the officer who is senior to me."

We learnt that Mr Taylor, about twenty-four, and a fully trained   5
child care officer with previous residential experience, was a strong and
hardworking member of the team. "He's quite an anxious worker, but
extremely good. A supervision session with him is most rewarding. And
he is very keen and always insists on having it. Supervision, however, is
priority, and we have an hour a week, but with John it tends to go over
the hour. In fact, the last one went on very much over the hour and I
was whacked at the end of it. Finished.

"When we first met for supervision, I asked him how he would like   6
it to go. And he preferred this fairly structured. He went through his
caseload, and then each week he brought whichever case was causing
the most anxiety. And this is a case which he has been dealing with
all through the change. It was referred this year by the N.S.P.C.C.
on a suggestion that a child was being ill-treated. The woman—I'll
call her Mrs Smith—is unmarried. Her eldest child is fostered out by
another authority and she does not discuss him at all. And then she has
a baby of fourteen months, the one who was brought to our attention.
And, when John visited, he found that she was pregnant again and
very anxious to have the child adopted, and keep the little boy, William,
who was then under a year. John was very concerned about the alleged
ill-treatment which apparently happened. William had been bruised
and taken into hospital. Mrs Smith said she let him fall when she was
depressed. She said she was feeling pretty low, and she did ill-treat the
child, neglect him.

"Then Mrs Smith was taken into hospital with high blood pressure.   7
She was very reluctant to be parted from William, who had great
difficulty in settling in the foster home. And then she had a little girl.
Up till then she hadn't wanted to keep the new baby, but, when she
was born, she decided she wanted to keep her. John had several calls
from her from the hospital, but on the last visit she said, No, she couldn't
keep her, because it wouldn't be practical. But she didn't want anyone
in the hospital to know that she wasn't keeping her and was going to
have her adopted. A week later, John brought her and the baby,
Caroline, home from hospital. He left Caroline with her and the man
she is now living with, while he went and collected William. He thought
it was better to get him back with his mother straight away.

"No, the father of Caroline is not the father of William. Mrs Smith   8
is Scottish, the father of William was a Nigerian, and the father of
Caroline is also a Nigerian.

"And John found that the father of Caroline is quite unfeeling   9
towards her, has absolutely no expressed emotion towards her whatso-
ever, whereas he's very good with the little boy and quite helpful there.
John had a painful afternoon. The mother was terribly upset. When
he went back with William, she was feeding Caroline, but the father
would have nothing to do with her. But the moment John went in with
William, he made a great fuss of him—the little boy who isn't his child.
Mrs Smith said her man didn't want Caroline. She was very tearful.
She wanted to keep her, but, if she kept her, Mr Nbongo was going to
walk out of the situation.

"In so far as the hospital is concerned, the baby has gone home with   10
her mother. But now she's in the residential nursery. Oh, dear, now I'm
so confused. I think the problem is whether John ought to encourage
this woman to keep Caroline, against the feeling of the man who is
so rejecting her. She is terribly torn. But John is also worried by the
original referral from the N.S.P.C.C. First she didn't want the baby,
then she did, but if she is going to keep her, it is quite likely that the
man will walk out."

Mrs Mansfield then outlined another difficult situation which had   11
occurred recently, when she had supported Mr Taylor in the way he
had handled another case. The senior had questioned Mr Taylor's
decision in terms of her administrative experience, but Mr Taylor had
been adamant that he would keep to his original plan. But when the
senior had taken it up with her, Mrs Mansfield had thought, " 'I see it
from John's angle, and that is where we block.' Perhaps" she continued,
"I'm over-identifying with the social work situation and not seeing
it in administrative terms. I feel torn. I have got to get a grip on myself,
see which side I'm on and look at it from both angles."

"So it sounds as if your anxiety on this case is something to do with   12
anticipating that there is going to be a similar sort of conflict between
the three of you on this case," said my colleague.

"Yes, I suppose that is one of the things I mean."   13

"But what does John feel is his role with Mrs Smith at present?"   14
asked a member.

"He sees himself as somebody on whom she is terribly dependent.   15
And she is. Extremely dependent on him. She rings the office a lot
and asks for him and she has been very depressed. He really is in an
acute dilemma. Should Caroline be with her, and are the two children
safe with her, particularly if she then loses her man?"

"And does he feel unable to make a decision with or without you?"   16

"At the moment he's not terribly sure of his own feelings. I don't   17
think he would have any hesitation in advising her to keep Caroline
if it weren't for the original referral. She suffers from depression and
can have quite violent tempers, but he says she is a very warm person
really, but had a very deprived background herself, and was brought
up in a Children's Home.

"He felt, when she asked him to take her home with Caroline, that   18
she was hoping, when the man saw her home with the baby, he would
agree that she could stay. But this wasn't so. He would have nothing
to do with her. John had to take the baby away. The father just said,
No, he couldn't cope with her, and Mrs Smith couldn't cope with her.
But in hospital she was so proud of her, and John says she's a lovely
baby. He was terribly taken with her. And she was heartbroken that
anyone in the ward should think she was going to have her adopted.
John asked her if she had told the medical social worker and she said,
'No, I don't want anyone to know.' And John hasn't told her yet."

"Sounds as if the M.S.W. gets identified with your senior somehow."   19

"When you were telling us about the difficulties in the whole de-   20
partment, you said your dilemma of feeling very split inside yourself
was not being able to marry up the administrative role with the casework one. Your team were saying you were one of the administrators,
and now you're feeling very much with John and one of them— being
pulled by various pressures either into one position or the other,
rather than knowing in yourself where you stand."

"Yes, I feel so torn in the situation. I have to get a grip on myself to   21
see which side I'm on and look at it from both angles."

"So you're worried about the supervision—that you've got identified   22
with John and that you're going to reinforce a split between him as a
caseworker and authority. And if you can't do something about this
yourself, how are you going to help him to reconcile the fact that while
he has some independence to make decisions on the casework, he is also
working within a structure?"

"He's extremely good, but the authority bit would be the angle   23
which would present problems for him."

"Like most of us."   24

"The whole point of supervision, surely, is to give people the op-   25
portunity to explore all alternatives and help them to make the decision
and then support them in it?"

"Correct me if I'm wrong, but I hear you say you feel so like John,   26
but ought to feel more like an administrator."

"I feel I'm identifying with John."   27

"Going back to the very heightened feelings about authority and   28
bringing the administrator and the supervisor together in yourself, it
seems that you anticipate the same battle coming into this case. It seems
to take you over to the extent that you lose a basic casework asump-
tion, and John loses it too. He starts talking about whether he should
advise Mrs Smith to give up her baby or not. But really it is her decision
to make, and his job to help her to make the right decision for her and
the baby. Poor woman, if she's got to choose between her man and her
baby. But you seem to feel that there is going to be an administrative
battle, whether she gives her up or not."

"I think he is trying to support Mrs Smith to make whatever decision   29
she wants, but he has seen another case where the baby was battered
and had severe bruising, and he is worried as to what might happen if
this man walked out and she got in a depressed state. He is carrying a
great deal of anxiety."

"This sort of case arouses so many feelings in everybody. But the   30
situation is different now, in that if the man does walk out, she has got
John. You say she has become very dependent on him. She may not
have to resort to that behaviour if she is getting regular attention."

"He has been very supportive to her over the last few months, but   31
he does carry a heavy caseload and there is a limit to what he can do
in this situation, if there is still a danger."

"So it is difficult for him to work out whether he should help her   32
to make her own decision or whether he ought to make an authoritarian
decision himself that the baby ought to be removed."

"But he has no grounds for removing the new baby, or the other one   33
now."

"Part of her grief seems to be that the father just doesn't want the baby."   34

"She said to John that he must take her away—for the moment   35
anyway."

"I think John feels very powerful with this woman. He could advise   36
her."

"Yes, he knows his client is very dependent on him and, if he chose   37
to exercise his power, he could persuade her."

"The enormity of the decision."   38

"How lovely to have the administrator make a decision . . . but left with 39
the enormity of one's own responsibility with no one else to blame . . ."

"I think he is very caught up in the pain of her feeling she has to part 40
with the baby. He was terribly affected. It was so painful."

"Not only is John experiencing a lot of pain with his client, which 41
you are also sharing with them, but he is also having difficulty with his
feelings about omnipotence. This is a difficulty for all child care workers
when the decisions are about things of this nature. They have such a
profound effect on the future of the child—one type of life or another.
Should he encourage one way or another? But whatever way Mrs Smith
makes the decision, he will have had some influence in it. But you have
an expectation that the senior is going to query the decision."

"I wonder why I feel this way."   42

"I wonder if it's to do with the case as well. Mrs Smith is afraid of the 43
M.S.W. knowing about her decision to part with the baby. She feels the
M.S.W., whatever she stands for, will be critical."

"Mrs Smith feels her basic problem is that you can't have one thing 44
without giving up another."

"The baby or the man."   45

"And, if you've got a terrible decision to make like this, it's often 46
easier if you push someone else into making it and then be angry with
them for making it that way."

"She's probably been putting terrific unconscious pressure on John 47
to make the decision, so then he gets very confused about her dependency on him and the previous neglect."

"And John has very strong feelings about wanting supervision. 48
And then you came along and said, 'What do you want?' He was bound
to put tremendous pressure on you to get you on his side, when there
was so much feeling about authority and the re-organisation. But,
with this case, it's so compounded. Which side? The child or the man?"

"One or t'other."   49

"And because of the other case, you start worrying which side the 50
senior will be on."

"You started your presentation about your difficulty of being a 51
supervisor; were you on the side of the workers or the side of the
administration; it was difficult to sort out where you belonged between
the two sides. Did you have to choose, or could you marry them up?"

"The baby or the man."   52

"So that's why I got the two cases confused—everything confused. 53
The clash of loyalties in the case and in the department."

"If I have one, I can't have the other."   54

"The client's problem got transmitted into the problem in the de- 55
partment and the problem in the department got transmitted into the
supervision. A real old jumble."

9

COMMENT

Mrs Mansfield felt the difficulties between the workers and management in the department were "tearing the team apart" (par. 2). She herself felt torn apart in her identification with the caseworkers and in trying to find an identification with the management. It was not surprising that it was extremely difficult for her to supervise a case in which the client was so torn apart between her feelings for her new baby and for her co-habitee, and, as we may guess, as she probably had been torn apart when she neglected the older child, William. And no wonder that Mr Taylor, as a member of the torn-apart team, found it particularly stressful working with Mrs Smith when she had this tearing-apart decision to make.

The pain was felt by Mr Taylor, Mrs Mansfield and the group. I have edited the transcript drastically, omitting the constant repetition of echoes of the pain (for example by Mrs Mansfield, pars. 9, 10, 15 etc.; by the group, 45, 46, 49, and 53).

Quite apart from the reality of the statutory function of protecting a neglected or ill-treated child, and the responsibility and the doubts when deciding to work with the family with the child still at home, rather than removing him, Mr Taylor's increased confusion was, I am sure, to do with the unconscious, or even conscious, pressure Mrs Smith put on him to help her make the decision (pars. 15-17, and 29), or even make it for her. In his turn he put pressure on Mrs Mansfield (par. 5) and at a time when both of them were still smarting about the difficulties over a previous decision. In her turn, Mrs Mansfield presented to the group her extreme confusion as to where her identification lay, regarding both the case and her position in the department.

It could be argued that the difficulty in the supervision of this case was just a reflection of what was going on in the department. Obviously it is partly so; but I do not think this is the whole truth. This example is, I think, of the reflection working both ways, of the feelings about the management getting into the work with the case, and of the case getting reflected back into the concern about how to handle the roles and relationships in the new working structure. Both were made worse by the other.

In this example, Mrs Mansfield showed more confusion between cases and between what were management problems and what were casework problems than the supervisors in the three previous examples. People are most in trouble when their inner world and the reality of the outside world reflect each other—i.e. when the fantasy or fear is confirmed by others. And it is more difficult to do good casework, or good supervision when the difficulties in the working structure reflect difficulties in the case, and vice versa.

Confusion (pars. 11, 12, 19 and 29) was the defence used in this example, as in the first one, although it was only partially effective, and the pain and anxiety continually crept through. One is left with even more pain when the confusion with the other case mentioned by Mrs Mansfield (pars. 11 and 29) is reduced and not allowed to influence this one.

It is very tempting to try to escape the pain of this situation by wondering if more work could have been done with Mr Nbongo previously. As the situation stood, Mrs Smith could rely on Mr Nbongo making the decision for her.* But the presentation of the case suggested he had been very unavailable as a client. As a co-habitee he came and went, as had the father of William. Mrs Smith apparently had difficulty in maintaining a relationship with men. Did she neglect William after one of Mr Nbongo's disappearances? It seems that in this crisis she was trying to solve two problems at once—how to hold her man, and how to care for her children adequately. But she found she had to make a choice between the two. Could some work have been done with the first, so that the second became less of a problem and not in opposition to the other?

We are always being beset by our own previous failures and those of workers whom we have succeeded. We don't know whether Mr Nbongo would have been prepared to work with Mr Taylor, even if offered a contract. This train of thought begs the issue of the situation as Mrs Mansfield presented it to the seminar.

POSTSCRIPT

Mrs Mansfield presented this case on two more occasions and the developments were interesting.

Mrs Smith did not have Caroline back, and eventually she was placed for adoption. At first, Mrs Smith refused to talk about her or show any interest in what was happening, but she showed some pleasure when told that the adoption placement had been finally made.

During this time there were two crises which Mr Taylor thought were connected. The first was that of a huge electricity bill, which apparently had been run up while she was in hospital and her co-habitee was not working. While Mr Taylor was working with her on this, having helped with a small down payment and having arranged for her to pay off the rest of the debt by instalments, she telephoned one day when he was out, leaving a message that William was in hospital. When he tried to visit on several occasions during the next few days, she was never there. At first the hospital was "cagey", and then said there had been a suspicion of battering.

However, when he went to the hospital for a case conference the

* When doing marital work it is often very obvious that one partner can easily relinquish a defence as long as he can rely on the other maintaining it.

following week, he learnt that there had been no battering, but, because of the history, the hospital had decided to admit the child when Mrs Smith had said he had been sick with heavy diarrhoea all over the weekend. She had been afraid to look after him any longer in case he got too weak and dehydrated. But, in fact, William had had no symptoms and had been in the best of health. They had kept him for ten days and Mrs Smith had visited every day. The main worry of the hospital was Mrs Smith's "stories". She was so tired because she had had such an "exhausting" weekend. " 'Well, my husband was along this weekend, and he brought our fourteen-year old daughter, and our eight-year old son and Caroline. I was so busy.' It was complete fantasy. It seemed the mother reached a pitch of anxiety where she brought him in and left him. And the hospital kept him in, to give her a break."

After this Mr Taylor felt less worried about Mrs Smith. She did not repeat the fantasy to him, but was much more relaxed, and eventually said that she took William to hospital because, " 'Well, I just felt frightened.'

"The hospital have said they will do the same thing again, because they feel meeting the cry for help in this way may prevent serious neglect in the future. They said she keeps him well—he was in beautiful condition."

This very positive approach of the hospital took a great deal of pressure off Mr Taylor, and he was able to clarify with Mrs Smith what he could, and could not, do for her; that he could not visit as often as he had done over the previous six months, but that she could ring him if she got frightened. He was then able to tell her of the pressures he was under, and she was able to say that she never realised he had so much to do.

Much of the work of these two seminars was about Mrs Mansfield helping her workers to set limits. The situation in the department remained difficult, but Mrs Mansfield's confusion grew less.

Summary

The supervisor, Mrs Mansfield, presented her supervisory problem in a very confused way (much more so than my drastic editing of the tape suggests). Firstly, she described the "open war" between the caseworkers and the administrators in the new social service department. This felt as if it were "tearing the team apart". Secondly, she described the problem of her worker, Mr Taylor, with a client, Mrs Smith, and of the "tearing apart" decision to be made whether or not she parted with her new baby for adoption. If Mrs Smith kept the baby, as she wanted to do, she was likely to lose her co-habitee, the father of the baby, and she would then be less supported than previously. And Mr Taylor had started working with her after she had admitted that she had neglected her fourteen-month old child. Thirdly, and tangentially, as it at first seemed, she described another difficult situation in which a senior administrative officer had tried to reverse a decision previously made by Mr Taylor on another child care case. Mrs Mansfield had supported Mr Taylor when he made the decision and had done so again in the argument with the administrator, but in the seminar she expressed great confusion as to where her identification should be—with the caseworkers or with the management. She felt torn between the two, as Mrs Smith felt torn between her man and her baby.

The Supervisor's Reflection. Because of their similarity, the feelings about the case and about the administrative situation became merged and compounded each other. As a result, the casework and supervisory problem was over-stated. *What decision should the supervisor make?* Should Mrs Smith keep the baby or not?

The degree and strength of the confusion indicated that the reflection process was working in two ways. Reflecting the difficulty in the newly amalgamated department as to who made what decisions with whom, Mrs Mansfield "forgot" that as regards this case it was the client's decision to make, there being no grounds for statutory removal of the baby. The work was about helping Mrs Smith to make the decision herself, however painful this might be. But the client was finding it very difficult to do this and was very dependent on Mr Taylor to make the decision for her. This was not spoken *The Worker's Reflection.* in so many words, but in his turn he presented his supervisor with similar behaviour so that she was the one left feeling she had to make the decision.

Mrs Mansfield was not fully conscious, until a member of the group pointed it out, of her fear of another battle with the administrator, but in this, as in many other cases, there would have been some relief from the client's pain about loss if the feeling could have been transferred into anger against someone in higher authority. The feeling of anger is often more bearable than the feeling of being left or of losing, because it helps to fill the awful gap and wards off despair.

The Group's Reflection. The group at first reflected the confusion and the typist had great difficulty in getting the recording of the seminar on to paper. To make it readable, I had to edit the discussion more drastically than the three previous examples. When we started to disentangle the various threads we were left with the client's pain and continued to echo this in the discussion. Our goodbyes were said in more muted terms than usual. The work in two subsequent seminars was indirectly about Mrs Mansfield's helping her workers to keep tighter boundaries round the intense feelings in this and other cases.

CHAPTER FIVE

APPLICATION

In the preceding chapter, the illustrations of the reflection process, of supervisory problems, and of how we in the Institute of Marital Studies work on these problems with groups of supervisors, clarify, I hope, my belief that useful conclusions about casework and casework supervision cannot be made unless there is some understanding of the personal involvement of the worker and of the supervisor,[1] including as well as their influence upon the client, how they are influenced by him. Use of the reflection process is only a small part of the supervisory process, but it is a vital part which affects other aspects of supervision.

If the supervisor accepts the premise that the worker is influenced as well as influencing, and can allow himself and his worker to be influenced without shame, he will work in a very different way from a supervisor who teaches on a less interactive basis. In this final chapter on application, I shall pick up a few points from the preceding text, which need some amplification, and which illustrate this difference.

One main difference between the two types of supervision is whether the supervisor primarily picks up the worker's transference or his countertransference (as defined on page 43). I will give two simple examples of this difference, distinguishing the two supervisors and types of supervision as (A) and (B).

A student opens a supervision session by saying he wants to discuss again the whole question of calling clients by their Christian names. Although his supervisor had previously told him that this was inappropriate, he has found himself calling a young man in his twenties, Paul. A supervisor (A), working more with the transference and thinking only in terms of the student's inappropriate behaviour towards clients in general—why he reduced their status in this way—might ask the student about his motives, or he might again make the point that clients should be addressed by their surnames.

A supervisor (B), working more on the interactive content of the interview and primarily with the countertransference, trusting the student's intelligence and that he had already grasped the general principle after the previous discussion on this subject, might ask him what Paul was like and how he felt in the interview in relation to him. It is quite likely that the student would reply in terms of feeling parental, or that the man felt so young he could not help calling him Paul. The supervisor might then usefully take up how strongly the client's emotional youth (or dependency?) was conveyed to the student, how he was influenced by it and how he responded to it. Further discussion might then be on whether this was a type of dependency and what type—i.e. the detail and not just the overall fact of the client's transference. And then he might say, "Gosh, I've been doing exactly the same thing and have also been calling him Paul while we have been talking." This way would be working more with the process of an actual interview, rather than in general terms of what should, or should not be done.

A second example of working with the process of an interview (and with the countertransference as a useful diagnostic guide) is when a student starts confessing in a supervisory session. He says he feels so ashamed, because he knows what he should have done. If the supervisor (A) has been giving out a lot of precepts, he may have pushed the student into feeling shame at the slightest misdemeanour. If supervisor (B) knows he has not been doing this, he will, rather than enquiring further into the student's shame, wonder whether the client has great shame but has not expressed it. What might the client's shame be about? If the student has reacted unconsciously to his unexpressed shame and is reflecting this, he will, unless this can come into conscious knowledge and he can be helped to "listen" for it in the next interview, continue to react unconsciously, probably by shaming the client.

The question for all supervisors is when to take up the transference reaction, when the countertransference one, and when to link the two. It could be argued that supervision primarily on the countertransference is appropriate only with experienced workers and only when the supervisor is well acquainted with their general standard of work. I can answer only in terms of my own practice.

I think there are no occasions when the supervisor should *work with* the transference of the worker. "Working with the transference" means exploring the feelings, and sometimes the genesis of those feelings, which lie behind the overt behaviour. Working with the transference means being a caseworker, and not a supervisor.

I think there are a few occasions when the supervisor can *draw attention* to an apparent transference reaction, but only when he is absolutely sure that it is a transference reaction and not a countertransference one—i.e. that it is pervasive over much of the work, cropping up inappropriately in case after case, and unrelated to the actual behaviour of many clients—and only in individual supervision, not in a group. If it is very serious, the supervisor may have to fail a student, or he may have to help him or a worker to ask for therapy for himself.

(There may be a few occasions when the supervisor, for want of another suitable person in the area, may have to relinquish the role of supervisor and temporarily become a therapist for a student, never a colleague, and only then if he is fully aware of the difficulties related to the change of role with which he will have to deal. Occasionally, and only very occasionally, this is a matter of expediency, not of choice, and I imagine it need happen only in rural areas.

Students may, of course, try to turn their supervisors into therapists. And I have noticed during recent years that some members in seminar groups of social workers studying casework have initially attempted to turn the group into a therapeutic one, and I have wondered if they have been allowed, or encouraged, to do this in previous training situations. I always stoutly resist this.)

If the transference is taken up in relation to one case, as described in the first example in this chapter, (A), and in conjunction with a homily as to how the student "should have responded, without enabling him to discover what factors in the client's psychopathology made it difficult for him so to respond, I do not actually help him; rather I only leave him feeling more wrong, stupid and inadequate than ever."[2]

I think there are many occasions when it is appropriate to work with the countertransference—i.e. the worker's reaction to a particular client and how he is influenced by him. I consider this is important information which I, as supervisor, need to know.

The longer the supervision continues, the more knowledge the supervisor has of the worker's habits—his norm, his strengths and his weaknesses. It becomes clearer what are his problems and what are problems with particular clients or types of clients—transference problems or countertransference reactions, conscious or unconscious. The supervisor is on very much surer ground in knowing whether the worker is carrying a reflection if he has supervised him over a period of time, either individually or in a group. But, at the beginning of this chapter, I deliberately chose examples of two situations which can often occur with students at the beginning of a placement, and I would use this method before being in a position of knowing their norm and their habits. While still in doubt, I would assume that, although all social workers, like everyone else, have their personality problems, they are, on the whole, less disturbed than many of their clients, and, until proved wrong, I would give them the benefit of that doubt.

I have four main reasons for working in this way. Firstly, I like to get the student or young worker as quickly as possible into the habit of knowing about his feeling reactions in interviews and not being ashamed of these. I hope a student can become much freer in doing this even during his first placement.

Secondly, it is a much less painful way of working. The supervisor is not conducting a critical exercise, and the worker is less likely to feel "wrong, stupid and inadequate", if the emphasis is not solely on him, but more on the interaction between him and another. If the supervisor is also watching for his own reflection and, when it occurs, brings this consciously into the discussion, again in relation to the client, he is, even more, taking the emphasis off the single person, and lessening the distance (I want to come back to this point) between himself and the worker.

Thirdly, because the countertransference is related to the transference, the supervisor is relating to this as well, *but not overtly*. (As I mentioned in the discussion of the two phenomena on page 36, the worker can react only from what is within him already; if it is conscious, he will be able to use the reaction; if it is unconscious, the reaction will use him.) The discussion about the clients' feelings and the attempt to get in touch with these during the supervision, particularly if the supervisor is acknowledging his feelings at the same time, will make it safer for the worker to know about his own. However, what the worker chooses to use of this discussion for himself is his own private business. Sometimes he will use this consciously and take his homework off, to work on it either as he travels to his next appointment, or, perhaps, in the bath at night. This will most often occur when he was aware of his reaction, or when the feeling which he reflected was very near to consciousness in the interview and came into consciousness during the supervision.

It will not happen if the troublesome feeling is strongly defended against and he thought the supervisor was talking nonsense in relation to the client.

More often the homework is not so conscious, but happens all the same. The discussion about the client and the reaction to the client may touch on a variety of unconscious fantasies. Quite a lot of resorting of psychic conflicts may go on beneath the surface.* (This is what happens in much therapy—the sort in which clients think nothing is happening for a long time, and then express surprise when they notice their behaviour has been imperceptibly changing and they have only become aware of it in retrospect. Some workers prefer crisis work when the client's defences are radically disturbed and have ceased to be effective.[3] The results can be dramatic. Others prefer working with clients when their defences are relatively stable, a much quieter reshuffle of the pieces in the unconscious jigsaw puzzle taking place.)

When the worker is doing his unconscious homework, or is trying to come to terms with feelings in his client and in himself, he will often

---

* "All the operations involved in coming-to-terms with oneself and the world, in face of continual change in both, are subsumed in Claude Bernard's fundamental concept of 'homeostasis'. This is essentially a Leibnizian concept . . .; homeostasis means achieving the optimum which is possible in particular circumstances—in short, 'making the best of things'. We have to recognise homeostatic endeavours at all levels of being, from molecular and cellular to social and cultural, all in intimate relation to each other.

"The deepest and most general forms of homeostasis proceed 'automatically' in all organisms submitted to stress, and involve depths and complexities about which we know all too little. Our deepest and most mysterious strengths are called forth from these levels."[4]

feel tired or out of sorts. In the Institute of Marital Studies, we have learnt from experience in running intensive residential courses on processes of interaction* that it is important to programme into the timetable as well as study groups in which the feelings about the course and the work have room for expression in public, "free" time for private homework as well.

In the examples given in this chapter, the. two students, one too easily calling a client by his Christian name, the other overcome with shame, may have needed to do their homework, consciously or unconsciously, and, no doubt, if one looked hard enough, one would find something in their personal histories, probably not so terrible or traumatic, which helped to determine their part in the interaction between themselves and their clients. The discussion of the client's feeling may bring them nearer to the basis of their own, but this is not the direct concern of the supervisor.

Usually the case which the student most often brings to supervision is the one which worries him most. This may be because of the extreme nature and difficulty of that case. But in early placements the cases have probably been carefully selected as not being too difficult, and the one which worries him most is usually the one which reflects some difficulty in his own personality, although in a much lesser degree than that expressed by the client. He will, therefore, be continually bringing back his own problem, and the supervisor continues to help him with it, but only *via the case*. In this way he links the countertransference to the transference.

Fourthly, once the supervisor takes the pressure off the individual (although knowing that a lot of individual work is going on), it is possible to take the work in the supervision further. When the supervisor is less critical, and therefore more supportive, the work can be looked at in more detail, as shown in the two examples (B) in this chapter. And I do not think the supervisors in the examples in chapter IV could have presented their difficulties so honestly, if they had not had previous experience of how the groups worked with the interactive process and how the presenting member was treated. Some of these groups were, in fact, very tough, and it would not be true to say that they did not, at times, occasion pain for the presenting supervisor and for others when the material and the discussion of it touched on something in themselves. Certainly, as one member expressed in the discussion of Mrs Anderson's work with Jack and Lorna Hill, their confusion often temporarily increased when they were trying to come to grips with some new idea, a disturbing feeling or an uncomfortable thought: "I mean, aren't there other ways of dealing with it?" said with a cry from the heart. But their difficulties in the supervision were taken

* This type of course is described in "Short Residential Courses for Postgraduate Social Workers".[5]

up in relation to the difficulties of the clients and not as a direct criticism, as one hopes they would work with their students and young workers.

This raises the question, however, whether, by going into more detail about the interaction, one might be attempting to take a young worker forward too quickly. I was interested, when surveying the literature on supervision, to read in a paper by Feldman, written in 1953,[6] that she thought the more sensitive students took longer to train. "Intuitive persons, who show quick insight into the behaviour of others, have been considered naturally endowed for this work, and as a rule have been welcomed into the field. Experience has shown that the fine sensitivity of these workers, although a great asset in one way, can also be a hindrance in training. Very sensitive to the meaning of the client's material they react too quickly and may overstimulate the clients, and, because of this, often 'lose' their cases. These workers seem to need, not less time in training because of their natural endowment, but, on the contrary, more."

I think this idea needs careful attention by supervisors. And Ackerman is saying something rather similar, when, talking about the dangers of the "sicker" students' acting out their own unconscious needs, he warns that the hazard for the client may be as great with the healthier ones, "who are less vigilant against their deeper impulses".[7]

The deeper impulses of the quick-learning and very sensitive student may be to work too fast for the client, and unconsciously aim to get the client to move at his own learning pace. These sensitive students are often adroit introjectors, more so than average. To get rid of the weight of feeling, they may show too much flair or intuition, and, in doing so, fail to work at the level the client has reached (page 47). When this happens it must be worked with in the supervision, mainly by the model the supervisor provides in not over-teaching, and in resisting the temptation to be too clever and to push the student onwards to be the best student ever trained—i.e., "by me—the product of my excellent supervision". As Searles says, "A too conscientious concern with making each supervisory hour useful to the student betrays the extent to which we have become intimidated "by the student's "infantile demandingness", probably accentuated by a reflection of the demands of the clients on him, and postpones the day when he will be able to resist these. "Here no amount of perceptive supervisory formulations will help, but rather one must become able to be reasonably unperturbed at the student's leaving one's office with a quite evident feeling that he is getting nothing from the supervision."[8]

Many cases get stuck or are lost on the transference reaction of the client to the worker, and on the failure of that worker to appreciate the nature of the feelings the client has for him. These students, very empathic and sensitive to the meaning of much of the clients' material, probably underestimate, like most new and inexperienced workers, the clients' feelings about their involvement with him, particularly if initially it looks so promising. Many clients have a difficulty in accepting their own ordinariness, and so do many clever students. It may be particularly difficult for the extraordinary student to help and to hold the extraordinary client. There is a lot to be said for the stereotype of the old-fashioned worker—plain with flat shoes.

But, however clever, however sensitive, everyone has their defences. It has been noticeable in the development of the three-week course we run for probation officers each year, on which the membership has reflected the development of practice in the service and Home Office recruitment programmes, that the general quality of work has improved over the years, but the defences that are used against unpalatable feelings have become much subtler; and the teaching problems on this course have become greater.

Defences are not to be despised. Young students on basic social work courses are, by the nature of the task, forced into maturing more quickly than some people in other occupations. Although I have taught only on a graduate course, on which the youngest student was twenty-two, I have always admired some of the younger ones who have resisted my and their supervisors' efforts to lead them where they were not ready to go, and, aware of what they themselves were at a particular point in time, refused to become "hot-house plants".

The difficulties of some students, trying to run before they can walk, does not, however, militate against my basic argument that it is more appropriate to supervise work of an interactive nature by a more interactive teaching method. In fact, I think it keeps the worker, whether he is a good, bad or average learner, more in touch with the needs of his client. This may help to meet the difficulty of the very "good" student, mentioned by Feldman. But I also think it is very important not to put workers in the position of later having to unlearn. Processes of interaction can be taught at a basic level and at a more advanced one. In the two examples at the beginning of this chapter, the supervisor who worked with the countertransference (B) went into more detail than the one who gave a homily on correct procedure, but the type of teaching described was still at a very basic level.

So the problem is not whether one does, or does not, supervise this type of interactive work in this way; but, within the whole process of providing a framework of security in which a new worker can develop and learn, the problem is where to "dangle the carrot"—to assess correctly the level to which the student is ready to reach. It requires skill to teach at an advanced level, but it requires more skill to teach well at a basic level and at the same time retain integrity to one's own subject and practice. (In some universities, the best teachers give the first-year introductory courses, laying a firm foundation in the subject, leaving the new assistant lecturer to take a more specialised third-year seminar).

I was suggesting earlier in this chapter that the supervisor, willing to show his own feeling reaction to clients and picking up his own reflection, will lessen the emotional distance between himself and his worker. But, paradoxically, it is not possible to have this closeness, unless there is some distance in other respects.

This question of distance in the supervisory situation is, I think, connected with the problem of how much autonomy to allow the worker, which was expressed by the supervisors in two of the examples given in chapter Four, and which was linked with their distrust of the value of what they had to offer. In both these situations (*Either/Or* and *The Management of the Thumping*), the supervisors reflected a distrust in the cases. But the expression of this problem was a way of phrasing the paradox—that it is not possible to be confident enough to have a close emotional interchange unless there is also distance—or, perhaps, one might say, 'difference'. If there is too much similarity there can be only fusion. If there is difference, and a boundary round that difference, there can be interaction.

This difference may be sought by creating a distance by an over-emphasis on autonomy (which is not synonymous with allowing the worker to take a professional responsibility for his own work). But much more profitable, I think, is a difference which is based on the supervisor's having more knowledge, more ability and more experience. His distance from the worker is more than just one step ahead. The latter situation is very uncomfortable for a supervisor and, unless acknowledged, results in generally defensive teaching. Some of the commonest manifestations of this are not being able to listen to the worker, not being free enough to pick up the emotional content of the work, not being able to tolerate the worker's confusion and muddle (part of any learning process), being too didactic, and too mistrustful of the worker's best efforts, undermining his developing individual style.

I do not think it is wise to minimise the importance of the teacher's grasp of his subject, his gift for teaching and his ability to communicate. The most satisfying teaching is when the teacher, retaining his integrity to his own skill, is stretched enough to keep him thinking— —pondering and puzzling—but secure in the knowledge of having something in reserve.

(It is one of the sadnesses in present day social work that workers do not stay long enough in their basic field jobs—in the clients' interest, in their own, and in that of those they supervise too soon before they have acquired more experience "under their belts". I hear that many young workers are promoted to positions of supervising-seniors, whether they want this position or not, and with even less than two years' experience behind them. In some authorities they are made, or encouraged, to give up their own casework completely, so that, quite apart from not improving their own skill, they are failing to maintain what they previously were starting to acquire. Unlike the professions in which the most skilled practitioners do the work requiring the most skill, leaving the more straightforward jobs to their juniors, much social work is very unprofessional. The skill that might have been developed, given more time, gets removed further and further away from the client, sometimes to a consultative post, sometimes a purely administrative one, higher and higher in the ever, it seems, expanding hierarchy, while the actual face-to-face work with the client, some of it excruciatingly difficult, is mainly done by the unqualified, or the newly qualified, whose position, in reality, is little more than that of an apprentice.)

The most important distance that the supervisor holds, however, is that he is literally and psychologically further from the client than the worker. This leaves him freer from anxiety and therefore able to think more clearly and more objectively. And this is so, whether or not the worker may be inherently more intelligent than the supervisor and potentially a better practitioner.[9]

One object used to maintain inappropriate distance between the supervisor and the worker is the report, which, it is often insisted, must be written and handed in before the supervisory session. "With a prepared report, one may confidently expect to get all the facts of the case in proper order, but unfortunately, more often than not, one would miss completely the worker's psychological involvement in his case which, we have found, is essential for understanding of the problem . . ."[10]

The report can distract the supervisor's attention from the worker's need of the moment and is "above all a further burdening of the elusively human essence in the client by this intrusively non-human element, . . . antithetical to the developments of the necessary depth of intimacy between the two participants."[11]

I prefer the report to be written after the supervisory session—a concise report for the file, when, together, the worker and I have discussed what was important in the interview. I deplore the waste of time of long process recordings, particularly as so few students can do them well, and, even more important, because they can so easily cut the supervisor off from the feeling tone of the interview. Once the interview gets on to paper, it acquires a structure and form it often did not have in reality. And relying too much on the written report precludes the supervisor from hearing the hesitations and what is forgotten and only recalled in the ensuing discussion—in itself diagnostically often very important. (In teaching seminars we ask members not to read from the files, although they may use these to look up some factual detail.) The reader may have noted that the group understood very much less of Mr Jones' work with Mr and Mrs Harris from his record (*The Management of the Thumping*), than they did from Mrs Elland's spontaneous report of what they had discussed in the supervision period. Verbally, and in the unconscious pressure he put on Mrs Elland, he was able to indicate where the difficulties lay. If the discussion had been limited to what was in the record, the supervision would have been much curtailed.

Verbatim records on tape and video-tape are now used more often by supervisors. The record can be very informative. But teaching methods *based solely on such objective methods* lose many important advantages offered in a more subjective and dynamic interplay between teacher and learner. There are things which the mechancial recording cannot give—technical alternatives the worker chose or discarded; the felt, but not acted upon, information the worker received; and the reflection. The verbal report may distort, but it tells the supervisor "the way the worker sees his experience . . . which leads to those aspects of the truth of what went on between him and the client that are truly important for the teaching and learning process." [12]

Some of these small aspects of the truth of what goes on between two individuals, worker and client, and the reflection of this in the adjacent relationship between worker and supervisor, have been the theme of this book. An acceptance, not just of the worker and his own individual style, but of the interactive process between him and his client, and between him and his supervisor, is, I believe, one of the most important aspects of supervision of casework *practice*. I emphasise the word, practice, because skill, as opposed to knowledge, cannot be acquired by reading, by either the worker or the supervisor.[13] Part of the price of acquiring this type of skill is that of being able to get close enough to be open to influence. It is a high price, but its payment is in the interest of the client's future well-being, the worker's future practice, and the supervisor's future supervision, and an attendant satisfaction for all three people.

26th April, 1974.

In 1972, we first discussed with the social work staff at the University of Exeter the ending of the workshop in its present form. We had new ideas and plans and needed to start on them. It was decided that the Institute of Marital Studies would withdraw in 1974 and that some of the Devon supervisors would, with members of the university staff, form a steering committee to plan and run a new workshop of their own. There were very mixed feelings about this—some resentment and some excitement—and, as one member said, "I knew you'd leave when you'd written it up." "But," added my colleague, when sadly we said goodbye, "perhaps our next task is to study how to supervise a worker who dare not know about his reflection and the influence his client has upon him."

APPENDIX ONE

POSTSCRIPT ON THE CASE OF
JACK AND LORNA HILL (continued)

"Then Jack came out of prison. But, before he came out, I, too, caught a little of my student's enthusiasm for helping him, and very much against my usual pattern of work, I decided to go to great lengths to get him a position where he could be trained as a heavy goods vehicle driver. I did a lot of this while he was in prison. And he caught the enthusiasm, but to get the tuition he had to go on a course.

"But, when he came out, he couldn't get a job while the course was still being arranged. But Lorna was saying, 'Well, it's all right as long as he works. That's the condition I'm back with him.' So Jack was between the devil and the deep blue sea. She got more and more angry and eventually they had a tremendous row. For once, however, he didn't go back to his mother, but he went to the Midlands instead. But the day after he'd gone off in this huff, the papers came through for him to take up the course and he couldn't be found. So the whole of that collapsed. And Lorna couldn't accept that her provocation had sent him away. A pay packet came from Jack from the Midlands— a sort of peace offering—but she was so angry that she just took the money and pretended there was no address on it.

"They stayed apart for three months and in that time Lorna got mixed up with a lot of dubious women, and then she decided she was a fool, and that she could get all sorts of things simply by 'lying on her back', as she put it. She came in one day and said to me, 'I'm a fool. Why do I stay with Jack, when all I have to do is to join up with a number of men? They'll give me money and I don't have to tell the Social Security.' And I said, 'You're coming to ask me if you can be a prostitute.' And she said, 'Well, that's what I'm going to do.' And I said, 'If you're going to do it, you do it, but I'm not giving you permission.' And we talked about how she came and tried to get permission.

"Well, she temporarily shacked up with another man who stayed with her for a couple of nights and gave her enough money to get the front room done up. He then disappeared and she never had anyone else.

"And then shortly after that, Jack came back from the Midlands, came into my office and said, 'Well, I want to go back to her.' He had got a labouring job. I told him I couldn't get the training place back, and this seemed a relief to him. He wanted to be a driver, but he's not very bright; he knows this, ran away from it and only came back when he was pretty sure the place was filled. He was astonished to find me pleased to see him. He expected me to be mad and was then non-plussed. But we re-established the relationship between us.

"So, after several interviews with them separately, he moved back. Lorna started dressing in her dolly-bird clothes again and looked very attractive.

"And Jack has been in work for four months continuously—unheard of for him—doing night work. But this makes Lorna feel neglected, and again she puts him in a quandary: he must earn enough money to keep her satisfied, but he can do this only on the night shift. Things are still very dodgy between them. When she goes too far with him, he now taunts her with having been a prostitute: however low he has been, she's now lower than he is.

"Yes, she went on the pill, but his previously not letting her go on it controlled her from being on the loose. He acted as her control, and he now taunts her with her lack of it. She's now faced with her own difficulty. But the night work now controls the sex they have.

"I'm afraid that she'll get him back off work. Then she can nag him, and this is the role she's best at—nagging, explosive, demanding. At present she's having fantasies about getting other lovers; Jack had said she's no good in bed, and she's saying she will show him.

"But I can take up an awful lot of this with her and months later she confronts something that has gone on in a previous interview.

"She didn't like my seeing Jack. 'I don't think you ought to see him,' she said. I said that it would be easier for me to let someone else see him, but I was not chucking him out. Did she want me to chuck her out? Did she want another officer? She came back a fortnight later and said she knew what it was like. If anyone could get them properly together . . . I'd better be the one to hang on. But she wasn't sure whether she liked it, but she laughed when she said she wasn't sure how often he'd come.

"We are already talking about the ending of the three-year order and that I will still be here. Usually, before the end of a long order like this, I say, 'You don't have to get into any more trouble.' She often threatens me she'll go shoplifting and says, 'You don't know how unhappy I am; others go shoplifting, they get away with it.' And then I usually say, 'If you go shoplifting, you'll lose your temper in Court and you won't get away with it. You'll probably go down.' I don't think she'll offend again, but I think this is all connected with her bringing so many waifs and strays to see me. 'Come and see my probation officer,' she says, testing me out. The most extraordinary characters she brings in; if I'll take them, I'll take her.

"And Jack isn't drinking any more and he isn't running back to Mum. But this makes Lorna furious. He's turned over this new leaf—and it's a hell of a new leaf when you think about it—and it's left Lorna holding

her own difficulties. She complains about Jack, but everybody she complains to says, 'What are you grumbling about? He's a good chap.
He's working, he's getting a regular pay packet and he gives you
regular money. And he's forgiven you for having another man.' But
she's got to have something to be angry about.

"She might, of course, at the end of the order, round on me, which
could be quite beneficial. I've had glimpses of it. I think she'll have
to lump much more anger on me and it'll come just before the end of
the order."

APPENDIX TWO

MEMBERSHIP OF SEMINARS FOR SUPERVISORS, 1965-1974

THE EXETER WORKSHOP, 1965-74

I.M.S. Staff
Miss C. Chapman, 1968-74
Miss J. Mattinson, 1971-74
Miss J. Newton, 1965-66
Mrs L. Pincus, 1966-67
Mr D. Woodhouse, 1965-71

University Staff
Mrs M. Collins, 1973-74
Miss U. Cormack, 1965-67
Miss J. Eastman, 1966-71
Mr W. Jordan, 1970-74
Miss J. Mattinson, 1965-69
Mr J. Nurse, 1972
Dr J. Packman, 1969-72

Supervisors
Mrs C. Abraham, 1971-73
Miss M. Anderson, 1965-67
Mr E. Anson, 1970
Miss R. Ayton, 1965-66
Miss R. Barker, 1969-71, 1974
Mr J. Birks, 1970-72
Mr J. Blight, 1971-72
Miss R. Bond, 1965-67
Miss P. Bowmer, 1965-66
Mrs M. Branch, 1970-71
Mr R. Brighton, 1968-69
Mr A. Brownbridge, 1965-68
Mrs R. Bryce, 1971-72
Mr G. Bubb, 1965
Miss L. Cafell, 1973-74
Miss A. Campbell, 1965-67, 1972
Miss R. Carswell, 1965-66
Mrs S. Chamney, 1966-68

Mrs L. Claiden, 1965-66
Mrs D. Clark, 1973-74
Miss D. Coombes, 1969-71
Mr W. Crouch, 1968
Mrs I. Dashwood, 1965-68
Mr R. Davies, 1968-69
Mr H. Dayes, 1969-72, 1974
Mr N. Dudley, 1969
Miss M. Eaton, 1970
Mr B. Ellis, 1969-72
Mr A. Fitzhenry, 1971-74
Mr G. Folland, 1971
Mr S. Ford, 1966-68
Mrs E. Fordham, 1965-66
Miss M. Freegard, 1965-69
Miss M. Fricker, 1974
Mr M. Furlong, 1974
Mr R. Furlong, 1972
Mr R. Green, 1972-74

Mr B. Grendon, 1970
Mr M. Guest, 1970
Mr R. Hall, 1973–74
Mr G. Halliday, 1965–68
Mr G. Hatchett, 1970
Miss H. Hill, 1966–68
Mr H. Hobbs, 1967, 1972
Mrs J. Homer, 1969
Miss S. Hudson, 1972–74
Mr P. Humphries, 1965
Mr P. Hunter, 1965
Mr D. Huxtable, 1972–73
Mr J. Huxtable, 1966–68
Mrs E. Jeanmaire, 1972–74
Miss J. Jenkins, 1974
Mrs M. Jenkins, 1965–66
Mr A. Johnson, 1968
Mr W. Jordan, 1969
Mrs P. Lawrenson, 1973
Miss M. Lenn, 1965–67
Mr B. Lillington, 1969
Mr J. Little, 1971
Mr A. Long, 1965, 1968–71
Mr J. McCann, 1971–74
Mr J. McCarthy, 1968–70
Mr R. McVay, 1970
Mrs M. Maggs, 1965
Mr A. May, 1971–74
Mr R. Mayston, 1970–72
Miss Y. Melville, 1970

Miss J. Midgley, 1967
Mr G. Mogridge ,1965
Mr J. Montgomery, 1973–74
Miss D. Morris, 1969
Mrs M. Munday, 1971
Mr J. Myers, 1972
Miss U. Parsons, 1965–70
Mr J. Phillpotts, 1970–71
Mr N. Pridham, 1968
Miss S. Randall, 1965–69
Miss M. Rossall, 1968
Mr M. Samuel, 1972–74
Mrs M. Scott, 1970–71
Mr C. Smith, 1969
Miss A. Stephens, 1969–71
Mr B. Stokes, 1970
Mr N. Stopard, 1966–67
Miss M. Suckling, 1965–66
Mr M. Thacker, 1968–70
Mr I. Thomas, 1966–68
Mr N. Tibbs, 1972–74
Miss R. Tregidga, 1967
Mr J. Tucker, 1971
Mrs J. Wagstaff, 1972–74
Mr N. Wakefield, 1973–74
Mr D. Webster, 1971
Miss S. White, 1968–69
Miss J. Williams, 1965–68
Mr F. Wingfield, 1969
Miss G. Yelland, 1965

I.M.S. EXTRAMURAL COURSE
SEMINAR FOR SUPERVISORS 1970–1972

I.M.S. Staff
Miss C. Chapman
Miss J. Mattinson

Supervisors
Mr D. Aitken
Miss E. Crook

Mrs B. Desborough
Miss M. Eeuwens
Mrs E. Heap

Miss R. Hillier	Miss A. O'Reilly
Miss M. Johnson	Mrs E. Pitman
Mr J. Lyons	Mr V. Young

LONDON BOROUGHS' TRAINING COMMITTEE
SEMINAR FOR SUPERVISORS 1970–1972

I.M.S. Staff
Mrs P. Coussell
Miss J. Mattinson

Supervisors

Miss M. Bayly	Mrs M. Holmes
Mr A. Briscoe	Mrs H. Kell
Miss K. Delaney	Miss A. Perrott
Mrs J. de Silva	Mr G. Shuttleworth
Miss A. Harling	Miss L. Tozer
Miss J. Henderson	Miss E. Watmore

SEMINAR FOR SUPERVISORS 1972–1974

I.M.S. Staff
Mrs P. Coussell
Miss J. Mattinson

Supervisors

Miss M. Cook	Mr D. Knight
Mr A. Darke	Mrs G. Loughran
Mr J. Day	Mr S. Rana
Miss E. Game	Miss M. Walker
Miss S. Jackson	Mr W. Wilkie

REFERENCES

Chapter One

1. SEARLES, H. F. "The Informational Value of the Supervisor's Emotional Experience." (1955) In *Collected Papers on Schizophrenia and Related Subjects*. The Hogarth Press and the Institute of Psycho-Analysis, 1965.
2. Ibid.
3. Guthrie, L. and Mattinson, J. *Brief Casework with a Marital Problem*. Institute of Marital Studies, 1971.
4. PINCUS, L. Ed. *Marriage: Studies in Emotional Conflict and Growth*. Methuen, 1960, Institute of Marital Studies, 1973.
5. WOODHOUSE, D. L. Spoken at a meeting with principal officers and supervisors in the Devon area, and staff of the sociology department of the University of Exeter, 7th May, 1964.
6. WATSON, J. D. *The Double Helix*. Weidenfeld and Nicolson, 1960.
7. GREY WALTER, W. *The Living Brain*. Duckworth, 1953.
8. SEARLES, H. F. op. cit.
9. Ibid.

Chapter Two

1. For example, BIESTEK, F. P. *The Casework Relationship*. George Allen and Unwin, 1961.
2. For example, TIMMS, N. *Social Casework Principles and Practice*. Routledge and Kegan Paul, 1964.
3. FERARD, N. L. and HUNNYBUN, N. K. *The Caseworker's Use of Relationships*. Tavistock, 1962.
4. Ibid.
5. For example, MOFFETT, J. *Concepts in Casework Treatment*. Library of Social Work, Routledge and Kegan Paul, 1970.
6. JORDAN, W. O. *Client-Worker Transactions*. Library of Social Work, Routledge and Kegan Paul, 1970.
7. JUNG, C. G. "Problems of Modern Psychotherapy" (1931). *The Collected Works*, Vol. **16**. Routledge and Kegan Paul, 1954.
8 FREUD, S. "Group Psychology and the Analysis of the Ego" (1921). Standard Ed., Vol. **XVIII** (1920-22), Hogarth Press and the Institute of Psycho-Analysis, 1955.
9. KRAPF, E. "Cold and Warmth in the Transference Experience". Internat. J. Psycho-Anal., **37**, 1956.
10. FREUD, S. Op. cit.
11. WINNICOTT, D. "Ego Distortion in Terms of True and False Self" (1960). In *Maturational Processes and the Facilitating Environment*. The Hogarth Press and the Institute of Psycho-Analysis, 1965.
12. FREUD, S. "On Narcissism" (1914). Collected Papers, Vol. **IV**. The Hogarth Press and the Institute of Psycho-Analysis, 1925.
13. FENICHEL, O. "The Counter-Phobic Attitude". *Internat. J. Psycho-Anal.*, Vol. **XX**, 1939.

148   THE REFLECTION PROCESS IN CASEWORK SUPERVISION

14. BALINT, M. *Thrills and Regressions*. The Hogath Press and the Institute of Psycho-Analysis, 1959.
15. MENZIES, I. E. P. "A Case-Study in the Functioning of Social Systems as a Defence against Anxiety". *Human Relations*, 13, No. 2, 1960.
16. Ibid.
17. Institute of Marital Studies. Follow-Up Study. Report not yet published.
18. FORDHAM, M. "Notes on the Transference". In *New Developments in Analytical Psychology*. Routledge and Kegan Paul, 1957.
19. GUNTRIP, H. "Psychotherapy and Psycho-Analysis". Lecture given at the Scientific Meeting at the Tavistock Centre, 22nd June, 1973.
20. RACKER, H. *Transference and Countertransference*. The Hogarth Press and the Institute of Psycho-Analysis, 1968.
21. FREUD, S. Taken from Bruckstück (Fragment) as translated by Jones, E. in Leland, E. H. and Jacob, S. *Psychiatric Dictionary*. Oxford University Press, 1940.
22. GREENSON, R. *The Technique and Practice of Pscyho-Analysis*. Vol. I. The Hogarth Press and the Institute of Psycho-Analysis, 1967.
23. JUNG, C. G. Lecture V (1935) in *Analytical Psychology: Its Theory and Practice*. Routledge and Kegan Paul, 1968.
24. JUNG, C. G. "The Therapeutic Value of Abreaction" (1921). *The Collected Works*, Vol. 16, op. cit.
25. JUNG, C. G. "Lecture V", op. cit.
26. HEIMANN, P. "Dynamics of Transference Interpretations". *Internat. J. Psycho-Anal.*, 37, 1956.
27. KRECH, D. et al. *Individual in Society*. McGraw Hill Book Co. Inc., 1962
28. The Institute of Marital Studies. *The Marital Relationship as a Focus for Casework*. The Institute of Marital Studies, 1962.
29. GORDON, R. "Transference as a Fulcrum of Analysis". J. Anal. Psych. 13, No. 2, 1968.
30. FREUD, S. "The Future Prospects of Psycho-Analytic Therapy" (1910). *Standard Ed.*, Vol. XI (1910). The Hogarth Press and the Institute of Psycho-Analysis, 1957.
31. For example, COHEN, M. B. "Countertransference and Anxiety". *Psychiatry*, 15, 1952.
32. HEIMANN, P. "On Countertransference". *Internat. J. Psycho-Anal.*, 31, 1950.
33. WINNICOTT, D. "Hate in the Countertransference". *Internat. J. Psycho-Anal.*, 30, 1949.
34. SEARLES, H. F., referring to Weigart, E. "Contribution to the Problem of Termination of Psycho-Analysis". *Psycho-Anal. Quart.*, 21, 1952, in "Oedipal Love in the Countertransference" (1959). In *Collected Papers on Schizophrenia and Related Subjects*, op. cit.
35. SEARLES, H. F. Ibid.
36. Ibid.
37. LOMAS, P. *True and False Experience*. Allen Lane, 1973.
38. JORDAN, W. O. Personal communication to author during a discussion on this point.

Chapter Three
1. *The Concise Oxford Dictionary.*
2. SEARLES, H. F. "The Informational Value of the Supervisor's Emotional Experience". Op. cit.
3. FORDHAM, M. "Technique and Countertransference". *J. Anal. Psych.*, **18**, No. 1, 1973.
4. Ibid.
5. SEARLES, H. F. Op. cit.

Chapter Four
1. MORTIMER, P. *The Pumpkin Eater.* Hutchinson, 1967.
2. BANNISTER, K. and PINCUS, L. *Shared Phantasy in Marital Problems.* Institute of Marital Studies, 1965.
3. Ibid.
4. FREUD, S. *Psychopathology of Everyday Life.* Benn, 1966.

Chapter Five
1. ACKERMAN, N. W. "Selected Problems in Supervised Analysis". *Psychiatry*, **16**, 1953.
2. SEARLES, H. F. "Problems of Psycho-Analytic Supervision" (1962). In *Collected Papers on Schizophrenia and Related Subjects*, op. cit.
3. CAPLAN, G. *An Approach to Community Mental Health.* Tavistock, 1961.
4. SACKS, O. *Awakenings.* Duckworth, 1973.
5. WOODHOUSE, D. L. "Short Residential Courses for Post-Graduate Social Workers". In GOSLING, R. et al. *The Use of Small Groups in Training.* Codicote and the Tavistock Institute of Medical Psychology, 1967.
6. FELDMAN, Y. et al. "One Aspect of Casework Training through Supervision". *Social Casework*, **34**, 1953.
7. ACKERMAN, N. W. Op. cit.
8. SEARLES, H. F. Op. cit.
9. Ibid.
10. BALINT, M. and E. *Psychotherapeutic Techniques in Medicine.* Tavistock, 1961.
11. Ibid.
12. EKSTEIN, R. and WALLERSTEIN, R. S. *The Teaching and Learning of Psychotherapy.* Internat. Universities Press, Inc., 1972.
13. BALINT, T. M. and E. Op. cit.